the alamo 1836

santa anna's texas campaign

STEPHEN HARDIN

the alamo 1836

santa anna's texas campaign

Praeger Illustrated Military History Series

PRAEGER

Westport, Connecticut
London

Library of Congress Cataloging-in-Publication Data
U.S. Cataloging-in-Publication Data is on file at the Library of Congress

British Library Cataloguing in Publication Data is available.

First published in paperback in 2001 by Osprey Publishing Limited, Elms Court,
Chapel Way, Botley, Oxford OX2 9LP. All rights reserved.

Copyright © 2004 by Osprey Publishing Limited

ISBN: 0-275-98460-5
ISSN: 1547-206X

Praeger Publishers, 88 Post Road West, Westport, CT 06881
An imprint of Greenwood Publishing Group, Inc.
www.praeger.com

Printed in China through World Print Ltd.

The paper used in this book complies with the Permanent Paper Standard issued
by the National Information Standards Organization (Z39.48-1984).

10 9 8 7 6 5 4 3 2 1

ILLUSTRATED BY: **Angus McBride**

CONTENTS

KEY TO MILITARY SYMBOLS

XXXXX	XXXX	XXX	XX	X
ARMY GROUP	ARMY	CORPS	DIVISION	BRIGADE
III	II	I		
REGIMENT	BATTALION	COMPANY	INFANTRY	CAVALRY
ARTILLERY	ARMOUR	MOTORIZED	AIRBORNE	SPECIAL FORCES

TEXAS

EXPECTS EVERY MAN TO DO HIS DUTY.

{ EXECUTIVE DEPARTMENT OF TEXAS. }

FELLOW-CITIZENS OF TEXAS,

The enemy are upon us! A strong force surrounds the walls of San Antonio, and threaten that Garrison with the sword. Our country imperiously demands the service of every patriotic arm, and longer to continue in a state of *apathy* will be *criminal.* Citizens of Texas, descendants of Washington, awake! arouse yourselves!! The question is now to be decided, are we to continue as freemen, or bow beneath the rod of military despotism. Shall we, without a struggle, sacrifice our fortunes, our lives and our liberties, or shall we imitate the example of our forefathers, and hurl destruction upon the hands of our oppressors? The eyes of the world are upon us! All friends of liberty and of the rights of men, are anxious spectators of our conflict; or deeply enlisted in our cause. Shall we disappoint their hopes and expectations? No; let us at once fly to our arms, march to the battle field, meet the foe, and give renewed evidence to the world, that the arms of freemen, uplifted in defence of their rights and liberties, are irresistible. "Now is the day and now is the hour," that Texas expects every man to do his duty. Let us shew ourselves worthy to be free, *and we shall be free.* Our brethren of the United States have, with a generosity and a devotion to liberty, unparalleled in the annals of men, offered us every assistance. We have arms, ammunition, clothing and provisions; all we have to do, is to sustain ourselves for the present. Rest assured that succors will reach us,' and that the people of the United States will not permit the chains of slavery to be rivetted on us.

Fellow-Citizens, your garrison at San Antonio is surrounded by more than twenty times their numbers. Will you see them perish by the hands of a mercenary soldiery, without an effort for their relief? They cannot sustain the seige more than thirty days; for the sake of humanity, before that time give them succor. Citizens of the east, your brethren of the Brazos and Colorado, expect your assistance, afford it, and check the march of the enemy and suffer not your own land to become the seat of war; without your immediate aid we cannot sustain the war. Fellow-citizens, I call upon you as your executive officer to "turn out;" it is your country that demands your help. He who longer slumbers on the volcano, must be a madman. He who refuses to aid his country in this, her hour of peril and danger is a traitor. All persons able to bear arms in Texas are called on to rendezvous at the town of Gonzales, with the least possible delay armed and equipped for battle. *Our rights and liberties must be protected* ; to the battle field march and save the country. An approving world smiles upon us, the God of battles is on our side, and victory awaits us.

Confidently believing that your energies will be sufficient for the occasion, and that your efforts will be ultimately successful.

I subscribe myself your fellow-citizen,

HENRY SMITH,

Governor.

ORIGINS OF THE CAMPAIGN

Stephen F. Austin was the first and most influential of the Texas *empresarios*. During the 1836 campaign, he was a Texas agent in the United States. There, he solicited money, volunteers, and sustenance for his adopted country. Following hostilities, he served as the Republic of Texas's first secretary of state. Sadly, he died in December 1836, not living to see the end of that epochal year in Texas history. (Courtesy of the Prints and Photograph Collection, The Center for American History, University of Texas at Austin)

The path of history, long and twisted, augured Antonio López de Santa Anna's Texas campaign. In 1820 Connecticut native Moses Austin applied for a land grant in Spanish Texas, on which he agreed to settle 300 American families. Moses died before effecting his enterprise, so the responsibilities of *empresario* (immigration agent) fell to his son, Stephen F. Austin. Munificent grants and deferred taxation attracted American settlers who were sincere in their pledges of loyalty to their adopted country. Nevertheless, deep-rooted American independence and republicanism prevented complete acquiescence to Hispanic religions and political institutions.

Dissention among government officials further frayed the bonds that connected American colonists to their new homeland. Upon his arrival in Texas in 1821, Austin discovered that Mexicans had declared their independence from Spain. Perforce, he rode to Mexico City to learn if victorious Mexicans would honor his father's contract with the Spaniards. In February 1823, the Mexican Congress confirmed Austin's grant. The following year Mexicans ratified the Constitution of 1824, patterned largely after the US 1787 Constitution. Unsurprisingly, this new development pleased American colonists. Two factions, however, grappled for control of the national soul. The conservative *centralistas* asserted that Mexico would never achieve unity unless the central government concentrated authority. Their liberal rivals – the *federalistas* – countered that unless power was disseminated among the states, the ruling elite would strangle the infant republic in its crib. Federalists, moreover, supported American colonization for the economic growth it fostered; the centralists indignantly opposed it. American settlers naturally sided with the *federalistas*.

In 1834 Santa Anna, the erstwhile liberal, emerged as a military dictator and overturned the Constitution of 1824. In October 1835 a new centralist congress dissolved state legislatures and transformed former states into military departments. When federalists resisted the centralist coup, Mexico plunged into civil war.

During the summer of 1835, a centralist force under General Martín Perfecto de Cos arrived in Texas and American colonists flocked to the federalist banner. One Texas lady expressed a common grievance: *The Mexican govt. is so weak & versatile & so susceptible of corruption, we are never safe from oppression & disappointment. He who can give the greatest bribe carries his point.*

The first clash came at Gonzales when centralist forces demanded a cannon that authorities had given the settlement years before. Instead, "Texians" – as American settlers now styled themselves – deployed the gun to drive the centralist detachment off the field. By the end of October the "Army of the People" had marched on San Antonio,

General Cos.

besieged the town, and cornered Cos and his 800-man force. On 5 December some 550 rebel troops stormed Béxar. On 10 December, after much bitter fighting, Cos surrendered. The Texians allowed Cos and his men to withdraw after receiving their assurance that never again would they take up arms against the Constitution of 1824. With that the Army of the People disbanded; most Texians returned home, believing the war was finished. Santa Anna was preparing to demonstrate just how wrong they were.

CHRONOLOGY

1834

Antonio López de Santa Anna, President of Mexico, overturns the federalist constitution of 1824 and establishes a centralist government.

1835

May, Santa Anna ruthlessly crushes a federalist revolt in the state of Zacatecas.

2 October, Texian settlers and Mexican troops clash at Gonzales, Texas, when Lt Francisco Castañeda attempts to repossess a cannon.

28 October, The Battle of Concepción. 92 Texians under James Bowie defeat around 400 Mexican troops in the first significant action of the war.

November, Texians besiege General Cos's Mexicans in San Antonio de Béxar.

5–9 December, The Texians storm Béxar. General Cos surrenders and agrees to withdraw his men south of the Rio Grande.

1836

16 February, Santa Anna crosses the Rio Grande. Urrea crosses down river the next day.

23 February, Santa Anna arrives in Béxar; Siege of the Alamo begins.

27 February, General Urrea surprises and routs a small Texian unit at San Patricio.

2 March, General Urrea ambushes a Texian force under James Grant at Agua Dulce Creek; Texian delegates declare Texas independence at Washington-on-the-Brazos.

6 March, Mexican assault troops storm the Alamo and kill all Texian combatants.

11 March, General Sam Houston arrives in Gonzales and takes command of the Alamo relief force.

13 March, Susannah Dickinson arrives in Gonzales to report the Alamo has fallen. Houston orders Gonzales burned and a retreat to the Colorado River. The Runaway Scrape begins.

17 March, Houston's army arrives at Burnham's Ferry on the Colorado River.

19 March, Houston moves his army down river to Beason's Crossing.

19–20 March, Battle of Coleto Creek. Following a bitter fight, Fannin surrenders his Goliad garrison.

23 March, Houston learns of Fannin's defeat at Coleto Creek.

26 March, Houston abandons the Colorado River line and retreats northward toward San Felipe de Austin.

27 March, Goliad Massacre. Following Santa Anna's direct order, Mexican soldiers execute Colonel Fannin and 344 of his men. 28 Texians escape to tell the tale. The news outrages the volunteers of Houston's army.

28 March, Texian army arrives at San Felipe.

29 March, Houston orders San Felipe abandoned; begins retreat to Groce's plantation.

30 March–12 April, Houston rests and drills the Texian army at Groce's Plantation.

17 April, Texian army takes the road to Harrisburg at the "forks of the road."

20 April, Texian artillery and cavalry skirmish with Santa Anna's troops. The clash is indecisive.

21 April, Houston's vengeful soldiers attack and rout Santa Anna's isolated detachment at San Jacinto. Texians slaughter 650 enemy troops and captures another 700. Santa Anna, however, manages to escape the field.

22 April, Texian troops capture Santa Anna.

26 April, The surviving members of the Mexican Army begin their retreat.

15 June, Lead elements of the Mexican Army cross the Rio Grande at Matamoros.

OPPOSING COMMANDERS

THE MEXICAN COMMANDERS

Antonio López de Santa Anna Pérez de Lebrón began his Texas campaign a national hero; he ended it a national disgrace. Those who knew the pliability of his principles would not have wondered at his meteoric plummet. Born into the Creole middle class in 1794, he became a cadet in the Spanish army in 1810. That same year rebel priest Miguel Hidalgo y Costilla began his struggle for Mexican independence from Spain. Resisting the revolutionary rhetoric, the young cadet cast his lot with the Royalist forces. Under the command of General Joaquín de Arrendondo he first traveled to Texas in 1813 to put down a revolt of Mexican revolutionaries and American filibusters. Arrendondo crushed the insurgents at the Medina River and Santa Anna earned a citation for bravery. Santa Anna took note as Arrendondo instituted a policy of mass executions to quash the rebellion. The 19-year-old student learned from the master that terror and intimidation were effective weapons. In 1820 Santa Anna won the rank of brevet captain and the following year that of brevet lieutenant colonel. Although promotion came quickly in Royalist ranks, Santa Anna perceived an impediment to his career ambitions: he was fighting on the losing side. In 1821 the 27-year-old colonel abandoned the Royalists and joined the rebels under General Agustín de Iturbide. Mexicans finally gained their independence later that year and in 1822 Iturbide – with delusions of Napoleonic grandeur – proclaimed himself emperor of Mexico. Santa Anna's timing had proven impeccable.

The ruthless colonel understood that in times of revolutionary turbulence an ambitious fellow had to do more than his duty; he must also keep abreast of the political climate. In a fledgling republic that was struggling to find its footing, one's political affiliations were not merely concerns of career advancement; they increasingly became matters of survival. Santa Anna broke with Iturbide, not because his rule was capricious and extravagant, but because the emperor snubbed him. In December 1822 Santa Anna led a coup against "Agustín I", who abdicated in March 1823. Ironically, Mexicans hailed Santa Anna as the champion of liberalism. He knew differently, of course, but relished his new role as the country's savior.

Following Iturbide's ousting, Santa Anna's star rose like a rocket. Serving briefly as the military governor of Yucatán, he resigned his commission to win election as the civil governor of Vera Cruz. In 1829 Spaniards attempted to reestablish hegemony over their former colony. Santa Anna brushed off his uniform, which now flourished general's epaulets, and quashed the Spanish invasion at Tampico. He bided his time and three years later the "Hero of Tampico" overthrew the

Generalissimo Antonío Lopez de Santa Anna Pérez de Lebrón rose to power as a federalist, but defected to the centralists to consolidate his power and influence. His reasons for ordering the pointless assault on the Alamo were political rather than military; his insistence on executing the Goliad prisoners sickened his subordinates and outraged world opinion; his slapdash deployment before the Battle of San Jacinto all but assured a Texian victory. (Courtesy of the Kevin R. Young Collection, Castroville, Texas)

CALIFORNIA

Ceded to USA
by Mexico
1848

UNITED STATES

Sold to USA
by Mexico 1853

Republic of Texas
1836–45

LOUISIANA

PACIFIC

LOWER CALIFORNIA

SONORA

CHIHUAHUA

COAHUILA & TEXAS

San Antonio
de Béxar

Galveston

New Orleans

Matamoros

Gulf
of
Mexico

SINALOA

DURANGO

NUEVO LEON

TAMAULIPAS

ZACATECAS

SAN LUIS POTOSI

TEPIC

1

JALISCO

2   3   4

Mexico
City

YUCATAN

COLIMA

MICHOACAN

5 6

7
8

VERACRUZ

CAMPECHE

TABASCO

GUERRERO

OAXACA

CHIAPAS

O C E A N

N

1. Aguascalientes
2. Guanajuato
3. Querétaro
4. Hidalgo
5. México
6. Morelos
7. Tlaxcala
8. Puebla

| 0 | 300 miles |
| 0 | 500 km |

government. Having "saved" the country again, he ran for president as a federalist and won election in 1833.

Although a putative liberal, in 1834 the president announced that Mexico was not ready for democracy, revoked the federalist Constitution of 1824, and dismissed the sitting congress. He had cut a Faustian bargain with the centralists. He would restore the privileges church and army officials had enjoyed under Spanish rule, *if* they backed his dictatorship. An unadulterated opportunist, Santa Anna possessed no core beliefs; he said what he must to win elections and then did what he must to remain in power. When Zacatecas federalists defied his centralist regime in 1835, Santa Anna slaughtered the state militia and implemented a pitiless campaign of subjugation. In December 1835, fresh from his victory over Zacatecan rebels, he arrived in San Luis Potosí to organize an army to crush the rebellious Texians. In this, his second campaign in Texas, he would follow the example of his old mentor Arredondo. Yet it would not suffice to simply suppress the

11

rebellion – he would do it in a way that advanced his political agenda and bolstered his reputation as "Hero of Tampico."

Santa Anna's second in command for the Texas campaign was **General Vicente Filisola**. Born in Italy, he joined the Spanish army at the age of 15. He came to New Spain (later Mexico) in 1811 to help the Royalists quell the Hidalgo Revolt. Later, however, he joined Iturbide and transferred his allegiance to the Mexican rebels. In 1833 he won appointment as commander of the Eastern Provincias Internas. While he was an able administrator and proven field commander, xenophobic Mexican officers never entirely forgave Filisola his foreign birth.

General José de Urrea commanded the eastern wing of the Mexican army. He fought many battles as a royalist, but he too switched to Iturbide. He was promoted colonel in 1834 and took command of the permanent regiment of Cuautla. The following year, as acting general, he fought Comanche raiders in Durango. He would be the only Mexican commander to emerge from the Texas campaign with his reputation intact.

Italian-born Vicente Filisola served as Santa Anna's second-in-command during the 1836 Texas campaign. Following Santa Anna's capture at San Jacinto, Filisola led the retreat of the Mexican Army. Following the war, many in the Mexican Army attempted to make him the scapegoat for the disastrous campaign. There is no doubt, however, that Santa Anna bore the lion's share of the blame. (Author's Collection)

THE TEXIAN COMMANDERS

Although an immensely different culture had shaped **Sam Houston**, he shared a number of traits with Santa Anna. Both sought acclaim and possessed confidence in their destiny. Also like the Mexican dictator, Houston's military achievements were the handmaidens to his political ambitions.

Born in Virginia in 1793, he was a year older than his future adversary. Following his father's death, the family moved to the Tennessee frontier. At age 15, Sam left home rather than suffer a clerk's routine. He found refuge with the Cherokee Indians who adopted him into their tribe. Thereafter, Houston shifted easily between the white and red worlds. When the War of 1812 began, Houston joined a company of US regulars and served during General Andrew Jackson's campaign against the Creek tribe, who had allied with the British. Leading a charge against Creek breastworks, the 21-year-old ensign achieved distinction at the battle of Horseshoe Bend. Although wounded and directed to stand down, Houston defied orders and, hobbling on a makeshift crutch, once more led his men into the fray. Astride the enemy's works, he took the bullet that nearly ended his life. Recovery was slow and painful, but he had gained a powerful advocate in Andrew Jackson. Clearly, Houston's grit and resolve made him a young man to watch.

Under Jackson's auspices, Houston became a player. Staying in the army following the war, he served as an Indian agent. In 1818 he won promotion to first lieutenant but soon afterward resigned his commission to study law. Remarkably, he gained admission to the bar later that same year. He practiced in Nashville and in 1821 won election as major general of the Tennessee militia. With "Old Hickory" in his corner, the practice of law would be but a stepping stone to public office.

As Jackson's protégé, Houston's ascent in the rough-and-tumble world of Tennessee politics was nothing less than spectacular. In 1823 he entered the House of Representatives where he served for two terms. In

General José Urrea led the Mexican division that swept the Texas coastal prairies. Winning victories at San Patricio, Agua Dulce, Refugio, and Coleto Creek, he boasted an unbroken string of triumphs against the Texian rebels and emerged as the most capable general of the war. (Courtesy of The Victoria College Photograph Archives)

ABOVE **Sam Houston as he appeared shortly after the Texas Revolution. Although "Old Sam Jacinto" emerged as Texas's greatest hero, more than a few veterans of the 1836 campaign maintained that he inflated his role to advance his political career. (Courtesy of the Prints and Photograph Collection, The Center for American History, University of Texas at Austin)**

RIGHT **An 1855 engraving that appeared in Charles Edwards Lester's *The Life of Sam Houston*. This spirited illustration portrays the young Houston after he had been wounded at Horseshoe Bend in 1814. He orders one of his men to pull a Creek arrow out of his leg. His gallantry at this battle caught the attention of General Andrew Jackson and began a life-long friendship. (Courtesy of The Victoria College Photograph Archives)**

1827 he took the governor's mansion at age 34. Tennesseans loved their youthful governor and re-elected him in 1829. Many spoke of him following President Jackson into the White House, but a cloud loomed over Houston's star. When his bride of three months left him, the humiliated governor resigned and fled the state to dwell among his Cherokee friends.

Houston's fall was even more sudden than his rise. Moreover, on this occasion Jackson could do nothing to prevent it. A broken man, he found solace with the Cherokees – and in the bottle. His disgusted Indian neighbors began calling him "Big Drunk". In 1832 President Jackson dispatched him to Mexican Texas to negotiate with a number of Indian tribes. Sam Houston would be one of many men to reinvent himself in Texas.

Upon his arrival he joined the War Party, a faction of American colonists agitating for independence from Mexico. In 1833 he served as a delegate to a convention that placed several stringent demands before the Mexican government. When open rebellion erupted in 1835, the provisional Texas government appointed him commander of the regular army. This force, however, existed only on paper. Moreover, volunteers openly mocked service in the regular army whose very name, one insisted, was "a bugbear to them." At any rate, militiamen grumbled, they had not required regulars to whip Cos at Béxar. Most Texians thought a regular army – and Houston – utterly superfluous.

As the 1836 campaign opened, Houston suffered from a number of liabilities. As a regular, he could not gain the confidence of egalitarian volunteers. His only military experience had been as a junior officer during the Creek campaign. True, he had functioned as Major General of the Tennessee militia, but that position was entirely honorary. He had never commanded an army. Indeed, he had not even stood on a battlefield for 22 years. On the face of it, Santa Anna had little cause for concern.

Nor did he worry about Houston's garrison commanders: J.C. Neill at Béxar and James W. Fannin at Goliad. Those garrisons were pitifully inadequate and the fortifications that they defended were, in Santa Anna's opinion, "hardly worthy of the name." In true Napoleonic style, he would crush these "perfidious foreigners" with strategic surprise and superior numbers.

OPPOSING ARMIES

This brass belt plate belonged to a *soldado* of the Morelos Battalion. The plate secured the crossed shoulder belts of a Mexican infantryman. It appears to be handmade, as the sides are slightly uneven. Below the scrolled letter "M" is a small hole that secured the chain for the musket vent pick. (Courtesy of the Houston Archeological Society)

THE MEXICAN ARMY OF OPERATIONS

Selfless heroism and shameful opportunism, a yearning for the old order and a thirst for independence, splendor and squalor – all were evident in Mexico; conflict and contention had left the people craving stability and a national identity. The chaos that enervated the fledgling republic also debilitated its army. Reeling from the excesses of Iturbide's regime, the nation hovered on the verge of bankruptcy. The Zacatecas campaign, while triumphant, had exhausted the treasury. Army planners understood that a near empty war chest required them to conduct the Texas campaign on a shoestring. Common *soldados*, of course, would shoulder the burden of this austerity policy.

The Mexican Army of Operations was impressive … on paper. In his itemized list of available forces, General Filisola placed the total number of effectives at 6,019. Yet, all his meticulous figures meant little once the army began it arduous trek northward. Tightfisted quartermasters allocated eight ounces of hardtack or toasted corn cake to each soldier per day, a pittance wholly inadequate to sustain a marching man under weight of musket and pack. Scarcity of water further sapped health and energy. Veterans might endure such privation, but recruits collapsed in throngs. The putative strength of a Mexican infantry battalion was eight companies of 80 men each. Yet during the 1836 campaign many companies fielded fewer than 40 *soldados*.

Mexican infantry battalions consisted of two types. The *permanentes*, as the name suggested, were permanent or regular troops. These units provided the core of veterans around which Santa Anna intended to build his army. *Activos*, federally funded territorial militia, augmented the full-time veterans. The *permanentes* took their names from heroes of the revolution against Spain. Hence, the Abasolo, Aldama, Allende, Galeana, Guerrero, Hidalgo, Jimenez, Landero, Matamoros, and Morelos battalions. The *activos*, reflecting their local origins, assumed the names of their hometowns or states, for example, the Toluca, San Luis, and Querétaro battalions. Most *activos* of the Yucatán Battalion were Mayan Indians, few of whom understood the instructions of their Spanish-speaking officers. Officials amalgamated one battalion from militiamen enlisted from Cordoba, Jalapa, and Orizaba. Perforce, it became *el Batallón Activo de Tres Villas* – the Active Battalion of Three Towns.

Its six center companies formed the fighting core of each battalion. Line troops or *fusileros* bore the brunt of most battles. Fusiliers carried the .75 caliber East India Pattern "Brown Bess," which in various patterns had performed as the standard British infantry firearm since 1722.

Two elite or "preferred" units supported the center companies. One company of *cazadores* – "light" troops – functioned as skirmishers or flankers. (Like the German *jäger, cazador* translates literally as "hunter".) Company commanders appear to have issued the .61 caliber Baker rifle to their finest marksmen. Most of the company, however, had to make do with special light infantry muskets. One grenadier company – *granaderos* – consisted of older veterans who acted as reserve troops. Like *fusileros*, the *granaderos* carried the "Brown Bess".

The well-trained and highly motivated *zapadores* (sappers) were the cream of the regular forces. Santa Anna valued them for their engineering skills, but also for their fighting ability. At the Alamo, for example, he deployed them as his tactical reserve.

Cavalry regiments boasted four basic units. Once in Texas, Mexican commanders frequently pressed auxiliary horsemen into service. These were centralist *rancheros* who lived in the area and knew the terrain. On occasion they also employed *presidiales*, troopers serving in one of the frontier forts (*presidios*). Famed as Indian fighters, they also proved able scouts and foragers. The *permanente* and *activo* units from the Mexican interior, however, served as the backbone of the mounted force.

The flaming bomb insignia identified the elite Mexican grenadiers. In all probability, this one fell off a shako. It was lost in the area of the boggy San Barnard River during the Mexican retreat following the Battle of San Jacinto. (Courtesy of the Houston Archeological Society)

Mexican cavalrymen wielded sabers, lances, and British Paget carbines. Cavalry regiments assumed the names of revolutionary battles and sieges. Consequently, the Cuautla, Dolores, Iguala, Palmar, Tampico, and Veracruz regiments.

Revolutionary instability decreased effectiveness throughout the entire army, but the artillery corps suffered the sharpest decline. Officials established the National Artillery Corps in 1824. By November 1833 they could no longer maintain the brigade of horse artillery and ordered its demobilization. Deficiency of funds disrupted regular maintenance. By 1836 the training of gunners mirrored the pathetic state of guns and carriages. As Santa Anna began his Texas campaign he had a mere 21 pieces of ordnance. Of the 17 field pieces at his disposal, he had seven 4-pdrs, four 6-pdrs, four 8-pdrs, and two 12-pdrs. For siege work, four 7-in. howitzers rounded out the total. Regulations authorized each artillery company a complement of 91 *soldados* and officers. In ideal conditions, a company could split into six squads to man six guns.

Mexican Presidial Trooper. Organized primarily for Indian defense, these hard-riding troopers manned the far-flung and frequently forgotten *presidios* (garrison stations) on Mexico's northern frontier. During the 1836 campaign they proved invaluable as scouts and light cavalry. (Gary Zaboly, illustrator, from *Texian Iliad*. Author's Collection)

For years, however, circumstances had been far from ideal. General Filisola noted that Captain Mariano Silva's company had but 62 men to service eight guns; Captain Agustín Terán's had six guns but only 60 men; likewise Lieutenant José Miramón had only 60 crewmen and six cannon under his command. Recall, moreover, that these figures reflected troop strength as the campaign began.

Although General Filisola did not list them in his order of battle, the *soldaderas* functioned as a virtual auxiliary corps. These were the soldiers' women: wives, mistresses, mothers, sisters, *curanderos* (folk healers), *lavanderas* (laundresses) and, naturally, the *putas* (whores). During the struggle for independence *soldaderas* had become a fixture of the Mexican army; by 1836 many a hardened campaigner would never dream of going to war without his woman. General Filisola complained about straggling family members, but the staff officers assured him that if they drove the *soldaderas* out of camp, the *soldados* would follow them. As the march continued and meager logistics broke down, *soldaderas* proved their worth as cooks, foragers, and even nurses. In the absence of a trained surgeon, a *soldadera* provided the only comfort a wounded man could expect.

Santa Anna's Army of Operations was a mass of contradictions and contrasts. Many officers were experienced professionals, but others had secured their rank through family connections and knew almost nothing of their profession. Generals drank French wine from cut crystal; *soldados* drank stagnant water out of mud holes. The *permanente* battalions marched and fought well. Even so, far too many unwilling draftees filled *activo* units. José Enrique de la Peña, a regular officer and one of Santa Anna's detractors, protested that recruits had been "snatched away from crafts and from agriculture, [including] many heads of families, who usually do not make good soldiers." These men knew little about the issues concerning faraway Texas and cared less. The Army of Operations had been, in Peña's discerning assessment, "created by bayonets and now had to be upheld by them." With each plodding step this army's liabilities revealed themselves. Before campaign's end they would become too glaring to ignore, too many to bear, and too entrenched to remedy.

THE TEXIAN ARMY

The armed rabble confronting Santa Anna in 1836 possessed almost no uniformity in unit integrity, direction, or organization. Custom demanded that each citizen-soldier join his militia unit in troubled times, but the man also took his leave the instant he deemed the threat had passed. Such practices alarmed Texas leaders; future Alamo commander William Barret Travis advised that "a mob can do wonders in a sudden burst of patriotism, but cannot be depended on as soldiers for a campaign."

Stephen F. Austin emphasized the "absolute necessity of organizing a regular army" and the provisional Texas government attempted to organize such a force. Modeled after the finest US regiments, Texian planners intended their regulars to be of the highest caliber. Sadly, the Texian rank-and-file did not share the politicians' passion for regulation.

Mississippi Volunteer. Recruits like this gleeful swain proved terrors to local civilians as well as their officers. Headstrong, independent, and proud, these fellows made fine fighters, but slothful soldiers. Still, the majority of those who fell at the Alamo and Goliad were recent arrivals from the "Old States". (Gary Zaboly, illustrator, from *Texian Iliad*. Author's Collection)

So intense was the egalitarian spirit and contempt for spit-and-polish professionals that, while the regular army enjoyed a surfeit of officers, it never attracted more than 100 enlisted men.

Santa Anna's army vastly outnumbered the rebel force. From the time the war began in October 1835 until it ended in April 1836, Texians never enlisted more than 3,700 troops. Fewer still ever concentrated in one place, at the same time, or under the command of a single commander. Instead, Texians parceled out their already paltry forces in penny packets.

The situation at the beginning of the 1836 campaign was typical. On 2 February 1836, Colonel Fannin arrived at Copano Bay with the Georgia Battalion and the two undersized companies of Burr H. Duval and Luis Guerra: some 200 men in total. Six companies met Fannin at Refugio; that added another 200 troops. Eighty volunteers camped on the Lavaca River later joined Fannin's Goliad garrison. Amasa Turner had mustered 100 volunteers at the mouth of the Brazos River and they also marched to rendezvous with Fannin at Goliad. Francis W. Johnson and James Grant shared command of 60 more volunteers at San Patricio yet, while nominally under Fannin's command, they typically acted independently. At Béxar, J.C. Neill faced the disheartening task of defending the town and the Alamo with 150 soldiers. In sum, some 790 citizen-soldiers – dispersed over a 150-mile front, without unity of command or concentration of force – faced an enemy 6,000-strong.

Understand, however, that these numbers were fluid. Indeed, this was a constant frustration for Texian officers; they never knew from one day to the next how many effectives they had at hand. Individual recruits might trickle into camp, but even as they arrived others dribbled out.

It would torture any acknowledged definition of the word to discuss the "organization" of the Texian army. Each volunteer attached himself to a company of like-minded acquaintances. Unit commanders attracted recruits by ties of kinship, force of personality, or the promise of wild escapades. One disgruntled German immigrant complained of another widely accepted method: *At the election of officers, the choice was not for the most worthy but for the one who could buy the most whiskey. It is no wonder, therefore, that orders were oftentimes not only ignored, but also laughed at; the captain commanded, and the soldier did as he pleased.*

A few companies functioned more like the sixteenth-century Scottish border reivers than regular soldiers. Texian civilians frequently had to fear "friendly" troops as much as those of the enemy. One resident condemned – in his own inimitable spelling – the conduct of volunteers passing through Gonzales. "The conduct of wild savages would be preferable to the Insults of such Canebols," he grumbled. Roving soldier gangs "pressed" animals, food, weapons, and other property. If they failed to coincide with their notions of strategy and tactics, company commanders frequently ignored the instructions of superior officers and plotted a unilateral course.

Texians were wonderful fighters, but poor soldiers. Once they sniffed gunpowder they were ferocious, but persuading them to stay around for battle regularly proved a problem. Independent and insubordinate, they were an officer's nightmare. Yet, volunteers demonstrated initiative, marksmanship, and remarkable physical courage. Jacksonian "common men," they mirrored the vices and the virtues of their age.

OPPOSING PLANS

SANTA ANNA'S PLANS

What an 1836 map revealed would have been obvious to any general worthy of his epaulettes. From the Mexican interior only two major roads led into Texas. El Camino Real wound northeastward through Béxar, Bastrop, Nacogdoches, San Augustine, and across the Sabine River into American Louisiana. The Atascosito Road stretched from Matamoros on the Rio Grande northward through San Patricio, Goliad, Victoria, San Felipe, and finally into the heart of the Texian settlements.

Yet, what was manifest to Santa Anna was equally clear to Texian leaders, who took steps to block these vital arteries. Two forts barred these approaches and each functioned as a frontier picket post: Presidio La Bahía at Goliad and the Alamo in Béxar.

The self-styled "Napoleon of the West" sought to emulate the French emperor. Santa Anna planned to strike swiftly, hurl his units along parallel roads, and achieve strategic surprise. Ignorant of his intentions, the rebels would disperse forces to check his multiple drives. Then, he would concentrate his battalions to deliver a hammer blow where the enemy was weakest.

The generalissimo anticipated ensnaring the rebels in a strategic pincer movement. On 16 February 1836, he crossed the Rio Grande on Camino Real and drove toward Béxar with the bulk of his army. The following day, General José Urrea forded down river at Matamoros with about 500 infantry and cavalry. Barreling up the Atascosito Road, his mission was to retake Goliad.

San Antonio de Béxar was the linchpin of Santa Anna's stratagem. "Béxar was held by the enemy," he rationalized, "and it was necessary to open the door to our future operations by taking it." Once he had reduced the Alamo, the town could serve as a supply depot, a stopover for weary *soldados*, and a springboard against rebel enclaves. His officers whispered, however, that more personal issues might have helped shape Santa Anna's plans. Some observed that Goliad – which controlled the entire Texas coastline – was of far more strategic importance than Béxar. Even so, Béxar was the political hub of Texas, its recapture vital to Santa Anna's political aspirations. But others surmised that the generalissimo's determination to occupy the town had more to do with maintaining his reputation. It had been the scene of General Cos's humiliating defeat in December. And Cos must be avenged to erase the insult to Mexican pride and prestige.

Once in Béxar, Santa Anna could weigh his options. If the out-numbered rebels rallied at some point further north, he could link up with Urrea, concentrate his forces, and trounce the enemy. If they broke

and ran – which was more likely – he'd simply unleash his lancers and hound these "land pirates" out of Texas once and for all.

HOUSTON'S PLANS

The factionalism that characterized the Texian government following the capture of Béxar excluded centralized planning. During the 1835 campaign, rebels were united against the centralist occupation, but now had to determine what they were fighting for. Some Tejanos and the old Texian settlers remained loyal to the Mexican Constitution of 1824. Governor Henry Smith, the head of the Texian provisional government, and General Houston advocated complete independence from Mexico. A third cabal, led by Francis W. Johnson and James Grant, plotted to forge a Republic of Northern Mexico that would be independent of both Mexico and Texas. Thus, the calamity facing Texians was not a lack of plans, but that too many were in motion concurrently.

Contributing to this chaotic atmosphere was the crack-brained Matamoros Expedition. Following the capture of Béxar, most Texian settlers returned to their homes. With no enemy to fight, American volunteers grew bored and restless. Fearing they would disperse, Philip Dimmitt, commander of the rebel garrison at Goliad, hatched a scheme to capture the port of Matamoros. He argued that it was a valuable source of revenue, which, if in Texian hands, would defray the cost of the war. The town might also serve as a base from which to launch hostilities into the Mexican interior. Although Dimmitt had spawned the expedition, Johnson and Grant soon ousted him and took over the venture.

Governor Smith's suspicions of Johnson and Grant were fully justified. They spoke openly of their plans for a Northern Mexican Republic. On 17 December Smith dispatched Houston, his political confrere and regular army commander, to Refugio to assume command of the operation. Yet, the men under Johnson and Grant were volunteers; Houston's regular army commission did not impress them one whit. Johnson wrote the provisional government barking his disdain

Ad Interim Governor Henry Smith. The beleaguered governor played a pivotal role in the Alamo debacle. It was he who revoked Houston's orders to abandon the fort. He also dispatched Travis and his cavalrymen to the Alamo to reinforce the hard-pressed Colonel J.C. Neill. The schism between Smith and the Council left Texas leaderless. The men of the Alamo and Goliad were to pay the cost of their neglect. (Courtesy of the Texas State Library and Archives Commission)

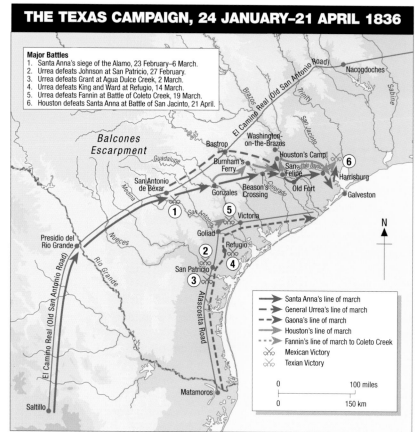

THE TEXAS CAMPAIGN, 24 JANUARY–21 APRIL 1836

Major Battles
1. Santa Anna's siege of the Alamo, 23 February–6 March.
2. Urrea defeats Johnson at San Patricio, 27 February.
3. Urrea defeats Grant at Agua Dulce Creek, 2 March.
4. Urrea defeats King and Ward at Refugio, 14 March.
5. Urrea defeats Fannin at Battle of Coleto Creek, 19 March.
6. Houston defeats Santa Anna at Battle of San Jacinto, 21 April.

Legend:
→ Santa Anna's line of march
–→ General Urrea's line of march
- - → Gaona's line of march
→ Houston's line of march
→ Fannin's line of march to Coleto Creek
⚔ Mexican Victory
⚔ Texian Victory

0 — 100 miles
0 — 150 km

for Houston. "You may rely on all going well," he insisted, "if we are not interfered with by officers of the regular army." The Matamoros volunteers had snubbed both the general ... and the governor.

This discord led to the collapse of Smith's government. Smith was the chief executive, but he functioned with the authority of the Council: representatives from the various Texas municipalities. Smith, now aware that he could not dominate the Matamoros Expedition, became its bitterest critic. The problem was that the Council continued to champion Johnson and Grant. On 10 January Smith angrily disbanded the Council; the Council responded by impeaching Smith. Ignoring his impeachment, Smith continued to issue orders. No one was certain who was actually in charge. While the Council backed the Matamoros Expedition, it could not agree on a commander. Johnson and Fannin each claimed the honor. Obligingly, the Council endorsed them both. By mid-January, most Council members had returned home. For all realistic purposes, Texas was without a government.

With Smith removed from the picture, Matamoros volunteers sent Houston packing. Smith doggedly clung to his title, but few but Houston really cared. On 28 January, he granted the "commander-in-chief" a furlough to adjust his "private business" and "treat with the Indians." But the furlough was merely a face-saving gesture. Hardly any Texians paid any attention to the pair. Consequently, when Santa Anna crossed the Rio Grande on 16 February, Houston was a general without a government, without an army, and without a clue. **23**

THE 1836 CAMPAIGN

SANTA ANNA'S ADVANCE

Company after company, battalion after battalion, regiment after regiment, snaked northward from San Luis Potosí. The dusty legions plodded through the Mexican desert. No matter, time was fleeting. The generalissimo was keen to move as fast as possible. "A long campaign would have undoubtedly consumed our resources and we would have been unable to renew them," Santa Anna explained. He also remembered the hellish Texas summer. From mid-May through late September temperatures regularly exceed 100°F. He concluded, therefore, that he had only four months to complete the campaign. If operations dragged on much beyond that, he worried that his *soldados* would "perish of hunger and the effects of the climate." Ironically, complacent Texian leaders believed that Santa Anna could not possibly arrive in Texas before the beginning of April. Actually, he hoped that the campaign would be finished by then.

So this would be a winter campaign: to European commanders frightful words that evoked bitter memories of Napoleon's disastrous Russian debacle. Nevertheless, Texas winters are typically mild, even balmy. The rare snow that does fall in southern Texas does not normally settle; snow that does lay might occur once a decade. Seldom does the thermometer even fall below freezing. But the winter of 1836 would be the coldest and wettest in living memory.

On 24 January, this misery was still in the *soldados*' future. By that date most of the army had arrived in Saltillo. His Excellency wished to inspect his troops, wanted them to see him. He ordered a grand review. Santa Anna, as he intended, dazzled all those who viewed him. How could any number of *norteamericano* rebels prevail against such a man?

After the review, the army continued the march northward. Between 26 and 28 January several battalions departed Saltillo. On 30 January, Santa Anna and his staff followed in their wake. In less than a week they had arrived in Monclova, fully120 miles to the north. On 9 February he and his staff departed that city and set out toward the Rio Grande. Between the two locations lay some of the harshest territory in North America. Ravenous soldiers soon forgot all the esprit de corps instilled by the grand review.

The "Napoleon of the West" expected his soldiers to live off the land, but seemed to have forgotten that the land in question was a desert. Men collapsed in droves. Officers found dozens of exhausted recruits lying along the road and employed munitions wagons and gun carriages to convey them.

Raiding Indians reminded *soldados* that Texian rebels were not the only enemies they had to fear. Both Comanches and Apaches hovered

Raiding tribesmen, such as this resplendent warrior, terrorized Mexican soldiers as they marched into Texas. Santa Anna dispatched presidial troopers to repress the Indian depredations. Their efforts were largely ineffective. (Courtesy of the Texas Memorial Museum, Austin, Texas)

Soldado, Tres Villas Battalion. This fellow barely endures the blizzard that struck in February 1836. The battalion formed part of General Urrea's division. It participated in the sweep of the Texas coastal prairies and saw action at Coleto Creek. On 27 March, the Tres Villas Battalion drew the unpleasant duty of shooting Fannin and most of his command. Although they carried out Santa Anna's barbarous directive, they did so much against their will. (Gary Zaboly, illustrator, from *Texian Iliad*. Author's Collection)

just beyond the horizon, darting in to steal, slay, and scalp. Santa Anna enjoined the *presidiales* to pursue, but they might as well have attempted to track the whirling tumbleweeds. One Mexican officer nursed bitter memories of repeated depredations. "[The Indians] were in the habit of roaming the camps where we had spent the previous night to see what could be found there," he noted, "sometimes venting their cruelty on those left behind or on deserters."

If the Indians proved unrelenting, so too did the barren terrain. The quartermasters had not provided the army with adequate water supplies. Desperate men drank what little a grudging desert afforded – even that in stagnant mud holes. The results were predictable; hundreds fell to dysentery and "tele", a fever brought on from ingesting rancid water.

Soldaderas and their children suffered most. What food and water remained went to the soldiers. Still, what man could stand idle and watch his children starve? General Filisola observed that *soldados* "experienced a burning thirst, and many of them, because they had helped their families, could not find a single drop to quench it." Even with soldiers giving them what water they could, the non-combatants endured unspeakable anguish. Filisola had never been enthusiastic about the pack of camp followers that slowed the pace and distracted the troops, but the plight of the women moved even him. "It broke one's heart to see all this," he lamented, "especially many women with children in their arms, almost dying of thirst, crying for water." But he knew there was nothing for it: "The tears that they were shedding were all that they could give them to drink."

Yet, despite every adversity, the Mexican soldiers pushed stoically forward. By 13 February, Santa Anna had arrived in the tiny village of Guerrero on the south bank of the Rio Grande. There he learned that his army was strung out for more than 300 miles. Units under General Joaquín Ramírez y Sesma were already across the river and bound for Béxar along El Camino Real. Others, however, lagged far behind. General Juan Andrade's cavalry, for example, had just left Monclova. Santa Anna could not afford to wait for them. His staff forded the river on 16 February. The stragglers would have to join him in Béxar.

While Santa Anna relaxed in Guerrero, the vanguard units of his army confronted a Texas phenomenon that natives of the state called a "blue-tailed norther". The term described a swiftly moving weather front that brought with it a rapid drop in temperature. Chilling rains, sleet, or hailstones typically accompanied a norther. On 13 February, Ramírez's men saw the livid sky ahead, but had no idea of what it meant.

They soon learned. Amid winds gusting up to forty miles an hour, the norther slammed into the *soldados* like canister shot. Pelting sleet stung faces and hands. When snow flurries replaced sleet, the men were initially relieved. Yet it continued to snow throughout the night. General

ABOVE **This is the Medina River crossing of Camino Real. Normally it is a picturesque stream – as it appears here. Yet in 1836 flood waters transformed the placid waterway into a treacherous torrent, checking General Joaquín Ramírez y Sesma's drive on San Antonio de Béxar. Had he been able to arrive in Béxar as planned he may well have been able to surprise the Texians before they gained the protection of the Alamo's walls. (Photo by Deborah Bloys Hardin, Author's Collection)**

ABOVE, RIGHT **Taking Possession of San Antonio, Santa Anna ordered his soldiers to hoist a red flag of no quarter atop the bell tower of San Fernando church. While the church has been extensively remodeled from its 1836 appearance, it nonetheless stands on the original site. Established as a parish church in 1793, it has remained in continuous use ever since. (Photo by Deborah Bloys Hardin, Author's Collection)**

Filisola observed "up to fifteen or sixteen inches of snow covered the ground." The troops gathered wood to build fires but, as Peña recounted, it accomplished little:

Officers, soldiers, women, and boys, all shivering, gathered around the fires; circumstances had made equals of us all, and the soldier could crowd against his officer without fear of being reprimanded. But these fires were insufficient, and furthermore, no one wanted to volunteer to find wood to keep them going. The wood, moreover, green and very wet, resisted the fire, which the snow suffocated. The snowfall increased and kept falling in great abundance, so continuous that at dawn it was knee-deep; it seemed as though it wished to subdue us beneath its weight. Indeed, one could not remain standing or sitting, much less lying down; those not taking care to shake their clothes frequently were numb with cold and, immobilized by the weight that had been added to their bodies, were obliged to beg the help of others in order to move, but help was given only with great reluctance.

For two days, the snow continued without pause. Peña insisted that it brought "dismay and sadness to the whole army." Morale plummeted alongside the mercury: "Even the most enthusiastic had let their hearts be frozen by these snows and were predicting dire results for our expedition."

When the blizzard abated, *soldados* brushed off the snow, buried their dead, and continued their march. Santa Anna and his staff quickly overtook Ramírez y Sesma's vanguard brigade on the Rio Frio. On 21 February they reached the south bank of the Medina River, the site of Arrendondo's triumph and Santa Anna's earliest glory. Despite

Mexican gunners lobbed howitzer shells like this into the Alamo compound throughout most of the 13-day siege. Travis recounted that "at least two hundred shells have fallen inside our works without having injured a single man." During their retreat, Mexicans artillerymen jettisoned this shell when they became mired in the soggy ground near the San Bernard River. The significance of the symbol etched into the shell's surface remains a mystery. (Courtesy of the Houston Archeological Society)

LEFT **Most scholars of the battle believe that Travis replied to Santa Anna's surrender demands with a shot from this long-barreled 18-pdr. During the siege it covered the southwest corner of the compound. Before their retreat, Mexican soldiers disabled the tube by knocking off the trunnions and the cascabel. Today the gun sits on the grounds of the Alamo. (Photo by Deborah Bloys Hardin, Author's Collection)**

the freakish weather, despite the virtual breakdown of logistics, despite the constant carping of all the naysayers, he had arrived within striking distance of Béxar. A little behind schedule perhaps, but still a formidable achievement. He had driven his troops like one possessed, they had suffered terribly, but that was of little consequence. He had gained his objective; he had achieved surprise. Now he would teach the rebels the price of treason.

But once again Texas weather intervened. The area east of the Balcones Escarpment is given to flash floods. Water comes tumbling off the Edwards Plateau with the fury of a tidal wave. Santa Anna had ordered Ramírez y Sesma to dart into Béxar with his dragoons and take the town before the rebels could take refuge behind the walls of the Alamo. Yet, high water tore down from the Hill Country turning the normally docile Medina River into an impassable torrent. A little past 5.00pm on 21 February, Ramírez y Sesma determined that the stream was too swollen to ford and had his dragoons stand down. Only a day's march from Béxar, Santa Anna might as well have been in Mexico City.

The water eventually subsided, allowing the advance to continue. On 23 February, riding at the head of his vanguard brigade, Santa Anna entered the Campo Santo (cemetery) a mile west of Béxar. He pulled up and from a safe distance observed as his infantry occupied the town. After some desultory skirmishing, his *soldados* took Béxar. The rebels, as His Excellency feared they would, retired inside the Alamo.

Santa Anna believed the time had come to send these "filibusters" a message. Ordering his men to hoist a red flag atop the bell tower of San Fernando church, he wished the rebels to understand that he would grant no quarter. With that apparent, he offered the garrison the chance to surrender – unconditionally. The Alamo commander, the 26-year-old William Barret Travis, informed the Mexican messenger that Santa Anna would have his answer in short order. Young Travis proved a man of his word. The reply came in the form of an 18-pound cannon ball. A terse response perhaps, but the dictator could not misconstrue its meaning.

With formalities out of the way, Santa Anna ordered his gunners to begin the protracted process of reducing the Alamo. Once they had knocked down the shielding walls, the rebel garrison would have no alternative but surrender. His Excellency opened the proceedings by lobbing four howitzer shells into the heart of the rebel compound. The siege of the Alamo had begun.

THE ALAMO GARRISON

His inability to take Béxar by a coup de main irritated Santa Anna, but he had achieved more surprise than he realized. In a 13 February letter to Governor Smith, Travis had opined that the centralists might arrive in Béxar as early as 15 March. Their appearance on 23 February thus came

ABOVE **William Barret Travis protested orders to reinforce the Alamo. Once there, however, he became certain that the fort was the "key to Texas." In his 24 February letter he swore that he would "never surrender or retreat." He never did. Travis's friend Wiley Martin purportedly sketched this likeness from life in December 1835, but the provenance is dubious. (Courtesy of DeGolyer Library, Southern Methodist University, Dallas, Texas)**

ABOVE, RIGHT **Among the Alamo's cannon was this gunade, a stubby, short-range naval gun of the period. Students of the battle have never been able to determine how it appeared at a post 150 miles from the nearest seaport. It saw action on the west wall. The gunade remains on the Alamo grounds. (Photo by Deborah Bloys Hardin, Author's Collection)**

as an unpleasant surprise. Travis understood that the Alamo could not hold without reinforcements. The fate of the fort now rested with Fannin at Goliad and any other Texian volunteers who might rally to their calls for assistance.

The weight of command fell squarely on the shoulders of young Travis. Ironically, he was garrison commander only by default. Although few today have ever heard of him, the true commander was **James Clinton Neill**. Following Cos's withdrawal in December 1835, the council named Neill garrison commander at Béxar. The Alamo held some 21 tubes of various calibers. With extensive artillery experience and a regular army commission, Neill was the natural post commander. Throughout January he set to work fortifying the mission fort on the outskirts of town. Major Green B. Jameson, the Alamo's chief engineer, mounted most of the ordnance on the walls. Writing to General Houston, he bragged that if the centralists were imprudent enough to assault the fort, the defenders could "whip 10 to 1 with our artillery." His predictions would prove excessively optimistic.

In a 14 January letter to Houston, Neill groused that his men were in a "torpid, defenseless condition." That same day he dispatched a grim message to Smith and the provisional government. "Unless we are reinforced and victualled," he asserted, "we must become an easy prey to the enemy."

By 17 January, Houston had begun to doubt the prudence of sustaining Neill's garrison in Béxar. Writing from Goliad on that date, he informed Smith that he had ordered Colonel James Bowie and a company of volunteers to San Antonio. Traditional misunderstanding of this letter's contents created the most persistent canard of the Alamo story: Houston ordered the fort abandoned; by willfully disobeying this order, the defenders were agents of their own destruction; had they only followed Houston's orders, they could have prevented their fate. Such is the persistent cant. As it normally is, the truth was far more intricate.

For the careful reader, Houston's own words reveal the reality of the matter: "Colonel Bowie will leave here in a few hours for Béxar with a detachment of from thirty to fifty men ... I have ordered the fortifications in the town of Béxar to be demolished, and, *if you think well of it*, I will remove all the cannon and other munitions of war to Gonzales and Copano, blow up the Alamo and abandon the place, as it will be impossible to keep up the Station with volunteers. [T]he sooner I can be *authorized* the better it will be for the country.**" [Author's emphasis]

Houston clearly wanted to raze the Alamo, but it is likewise obvious that he was seeking Smith's permission to do so. There were few issues upon which Smith and the council could concur. Nevertheless, both the governor and the council were in agreement that they must maintain the Alamo. Ultimately, Smith refused to approve Houston's proposal.

On 19 January, Bowie rode into the Alamo. What he saw impressed him. The old mission had begun to take on the appearance of a real fort. Neill's arguments and leadership electrified Bowie. "I cannot eulogize the conduct & character of Col. Neill too highly," he wrote Smith; "no other man in the army could have kept men at this post, under the neglect they have experienced." He declared that he and Neill had resolved to "die in these ditches" before they would surrender the post. Bowie's letter confirmed the governor's view of the defensibility of the Alamo. Smith and the council had already concluded that Béxar could not go undefended and Bowie's judgment only strengthened his determination. Rejecting Houston's plan, Smith prepared to funnel additional troops and provisions to the Alamo.

Houston demonstrably did not dispatch "orders" to abandon the Alamo only to have Neill ignore them. In brief, Houston had asked for permission to evacuate the post. The politicians considered his request; the answer was an unequivocal "No." After the Texas government fell apart, both Governor Smith and the council directed Neill to hold his post. There was no directive from Houston to evacuate the fort for Neill to disobey.

Neill complained that "for want of horses," he could not even "send out a small spy company." Now fully committed to maintaining the Béxar garrison, Smith directed Lieutenant Colonel William B. Travis to take his "Legion of Cavalry" and report to Neill. A crestfallen Travis pleaded with Smith to reconsider. He even threatened to resign his commission. Smith, however, knew the measure of his man. As Smith knew he would, Travis obeyed orders and dutifully made his way to Béxar at the head of his 30-horse "legion".

J.C. Neill welcomed the reinforcements as they trickled into Béxar. On 3 February, Travis and his cavalry contingent reached the Alamo. Although the cavalry officer had traveled to his new duty station under duress, he soon became committed to Neill and the garrison. Not long afterward he took to calling the Alamo the "key to Texas." Curious, that Santa Anna and Travis should have selected similar metaphors to describe Béxar's strategic significance. Then, on or about 8 February, the Alamo garrison received the biggest boost to their morale. On that date a group of American volunteers arrived; among them was none other than the redoubtable David Crockett.

On the day that he rode into the Alamo, **David Crockett** was already a marvel of the American frontier. At 49 years of age he had established a reputation as an Indian fighter, a bear hunter (he claimed to have bagged 105 in a single season), and a three-term US congressman. He

Contrary to the popular culture stereotype, David Crockett preferred conventional attire to buckskins. During his time in Texas, one lady insisted that he was "dressed like a gentleman and not a backwoodsman." One might easily believe that when viewing this 1834 portrait. (Courtesy of the National Portrait Gallery, Smithsonian Institution, Washington, D.C. On loan from Katherine Bradford in honor of her mother, Dorothy W. Bradford)

never tired of parading his humble origins, his lack of privilege, even his lack of schooling. During his time as a Tennessee magistrate, Crockett – who always signed his name "David" and seemingly never encouraged anyone to call him "Davy" – assured voters that he "relied on natural born sense, and not on law learning to guide me." He turned traditional politics on its ear. Rather than appeal to his knowledge and experience, Crockett urged constituents to vote for him because he had none. And they did.

Crockett personified the common man. His tall tales and down-home manners bolstered his growing reputation as the "Lion of the West". His fame was such that his name entered the vernacular. If an individual or object was impressive enough to challenge his stature, folks said it was "a sin to Crockett." A typical exchange might unfold along these lines:

"Lordy, Zeb, that's the biggest steamboat I ever seen on this river!"

"Yep, Luther, she's a big 'un alright. A regular sin to Crockett."

But not even the "Lion of the West" could avoid the snares of politics. He overplayed his hand when he opposed the Jackson political machine. "Old Hickory" brought his considerable power to bear against his erstwhile ally and voters rejected him. Bitter at losing what he considered a rigged election, Crockett told his former constituents that they "might go to Hell" and he "would go to Texas."

And so he did. Upon Crockett's arrival in Béxar, Neill's men welcomed him like a visiting dignitary, even hosting a *fandango* in his honor. Crockett, however, refused to accept military rank. Instead, he insisted he would serve as a "high private." By shunning status he sided with the volunteers, a powerful voting block. Again in his element, Crockett could manage without the formal title; he held these men in the palm of his hand.

On 14 February the departure of Colonel Neill dampened the mood. He had received word that illness had struck his family; they desperately needed him at home. While he vowed to return within 20 days, his troops hated to see him go. They were also apprehensive over the transfer of command to the headstrong Travis. Neill did not mean to snub the older, more experienced Bowie, but Travis held a regular commission. Bowie was merely an elected colonel of volunteers. The garrison certainly admired Crockett, but he was new to Texas and had no wish to command. Travis emerged as the only serious contender. Transferring command to Travis, Neill rode out of the Alamo and into anonymity.

Historians have been uncharitable in their assessment of J.C. Neill. Despite the neglect of the provisional government, he kept the garrison intact and maintained morale. He worked assiduously to transform the crumbling mission into a fort. Santa Anna arrived before Neill could return to command. Thus, it was Travis who fought the battle and won lasting fame. Even so, had it not been for Neill there would have been no garrison for Travis to inherit, no fort, no epic stand, and no entry into myth and legend.

Accustomed to electing their officers, the volunteers resented having this regular foisted upon them. Neill's maturity, judgement, and proven ability had won the respect of both regulars and volunteers. Travis, however, was an unknown quantity. The volunteers demanded an

Land speculator, adventurer, and con-artist, James Bowie was already famous before the Alamo battle. He committed himself to its defense, writing to Governor Smith that he preferred to "die in these ditches" rather than abandon the post. This portrait did not surface until 1889. The Bowie family steadfastly maintained that the artist painted it from life, an assertion that is far from certain. (Courtesy of the Prints and Photograph Collection, Center for American History, University of Texas at Austin)

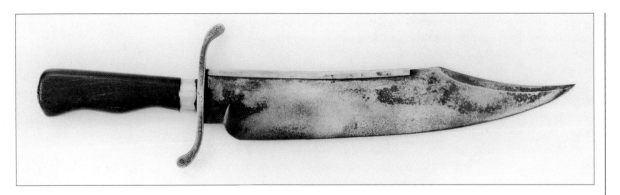

During the 1830s "Bowie" was the generic term for any large fighting knife. Blades – even those identified with Bowie himself – came in various shapes and sizes. Nevertheless, the one depicted here is the classic Bowie knife. Note the clipped point, the brass quillons, and brass strip on the back of its 13³/₄in. blade. Myth clouds the origins of the Bowie design, but its association with the Alamo defender and his exploits established its repute. (Courtesy of Joseph Musso)

election, and Travis submitted to their will. The garrison cast its votes along service lines: regulars voted for Travis, volunteers for Bowie.

At this juncture the vagaries of Bowie's personality took a hand in events. At age 39, **James Bowie** had already achieved a reputation along the Mississippi River valley. A true son of the frontier, while still a boy he reputedly broke wild horses, trapped bears, and even rode alligators. Bowie, along with brother Rezin, first made his mark as a slave trader. An opportunist of the first order, he was always on the make for an honest, or even the occasional dishonest, buck. Bowie was not above forging land certificates or participating in wholesale land fraud. Such shady dealings won the Bowie brothers the enmity of several powerful men. In 1827 James became embroiled in the infamous "Sandbar Fight" just outside Natchez, Mississippi. After being shot and stabbed numerous times, Bowie drew his "large butcher knife" and slew his antagonist, Norris Wright. Bowie's wounds nearly killed him, but the Sandbar imbroglio established him as the South's most accomplished knife fighter. Scholars debate the origins of his notorious knife, but none deny that its connection with Bowie made it part of the American lexicon. In no time, dandies and cutthroats throughout the South were demanding that blacksmiths fashion them a "Bowie" knife.

In 1830 Bowie rode to Texas seeking new prospects and found them in abundance. Arriving in Béxar, Bowie presented himself as a gentleman of style and substance. This sham won him the hand of Ursula de Veramendi, the daughter of a wealthy and influential Tejano family. Bowie learned Spanish, brazenly employed family connections, and soon had a foot in both the Tejano and Texian communities. Family ties snapped, however, when a cholera epidemic swept off his father-in-law, his mother-in-law, and his wife. As affairs between the Mexican government and American colonists deteriorated, Bowie increasingly identified with Houston, Smith, and the War Party.

When the fighting erupted in 1835 Bowie demonstrated a shrewd tactical ability at the battle of Concepción, but hesitated to follow orders that did not further his personal agenda. Even so, volunteers admired the famed knife fighter. He possessed a rough-and-tumble quality that attracted those of a similar ilk. His friend Caiaphas Ham left a fair description: "He was a foe no one dared to undervalue, and many feared. When unexcited there was a calm seriousness shadowing his countenance which gave assurance of great will power, unbending firmness of purpose, and unflinching courage. When fired by anger his face bore the semblance of an enraged tiger."

Like Bowie, **William Barret Travis** also had an abrasive personality. J.H. Kuykendall, a friend and former law clerk, conceded that his old boss was "able and honest," but that he was also "loud and somewhat harsh" and possessed a "brusque manner." Those traits, along with self-confidence which many thought arrogance, led Kuykendall to conclude that Travis "was not a very popular man." His subordinates acknowledged his competence and, in time, came to trust his leadership, but seldom could they admit to liking him.

Travis had been a lad of astounding promise. By age 20 he had passed the Alabama bar and was practicing law. He supplemented his earnings by teaching at a local academy where he became enamored of Rosanna Cato, one of his students. The couple married on 26 October 1826. But it appears that a full two months earlier Travis's 16-year-old bride had presented him with a bouncing baby boy.

But family life failed to meet expectation. Wages never kept pace with expenditures; it became increasingly difficult to keep up appearances. Finally, in 1830, he abandoned his son and wife – now pregnant with his second child – and booted his horse toward Texas.

Travis arrived in that Mexican province early in 1831. Here he would rebuild his fortune as well as his self-esteem. *Empresario* Austin awarded him a land grant, but on his application Travis listed his marital status as "single". Still in denial, he wished to forget his old life and begin anew in Texas. He hung out his shingle and soon built a thriving law practice. He became active in War Party politics. In 1832 he found himself behind bars for his radical activities, but Mexican authorities (under threat from a Texian mob) thought it best to release him. Travis never relented in his diatribes against the Mexican government.

When war began he rushed to the colors and served with distinction during the Siege of Béxar. On 19 December 1835 the council created the Legion of Cavalry. The following day the delegates unanimously named Travis commander with the rank of lieutenant colonel. By temperament and inclination he was a cavalier. Hence, his resistance to trotting off to the Alamo in command of a corporal's guard. Then Neill went on furlough and left him in command. Travis, the cavalryman, found even the temporary command of an artillery post a bitter pill. Bowie, moreover, was about to make a bad situation even worse.

The night following the election, Bowie mortified Béxar residents with a besotted carousal. In an angry letter to the governor, Travis complained that Bowie's behavior placed him in an "awkward situation." He assured Smith that he refused to assume responsibility "for the drunken irregularities of any man" – not even the mighty Jim Bowie.

Fortunately, this affront did not produce a lasting breach between the two commanders. Bowie had been an ass, and he knew it. When sober, he approached Travis with an offer. Bowie would command the volunteers, Travis the regulars. Until Neill returned, both of them would sign orders and correspondence. Travis saw this gesture as an obvious peace overture on Bowie's part, and accepted the compromise in the same spirit. Whatever their faults, Travis knew that he needed Bowie and his obstreperous volunteers.

That became all the more apparent when centralist forces occupied Béxar on 23 February. Although Tejano scouts had informed the co-commanders that Santa Anna had crossed the Rio Grande, neither of

Texian Leather Stocking. While these outrageously clad scions of the backwoods attracted much comment from their more conventionally attired comrades, they remained a distinct minority. The vast majority of Texian revolutionaries would have resembled Oliver Twist far more than Natty Bumpo. Even so, Mexican soldiers working within two hundred yards of the Alamo walls learned to fear the deadly marksmanship of fellows such as this. (Gary Zaboly, illustrator, from *Texian Iliad*. Author's Collection).

them believed that he could arrive so quickly. By much hard marching, Santa Anna had stolen a march on the Texians.

SIEGE

During the first days of the siege, Alamo defenders exuded confidence. If the centralists made a frontal assault, they could inflict heavy losses with rifles and artillery. Far from being bent on self-sacrifice, Travis and the garrison honestly believed that they could hold the fort – at least until reinforcements arrived.

Mexican officers took another view. They never worried about the Alamo itself; when its food ran out, its fall was certain. Peña dismissed the fort as "an irregular fortification without flank fires which a wise general would have taken with insignificant losses." Filisola agreed: "By merely placing twenty artillery pieces properly, that poor wall could not have withstood one hour of cannon fire without being reduced to rubble."

TEXAS
EXPECTS EVERY MAN TO DO HIS DUTY.

EXECUTIVE DEPARTMENT OF TEXAS.

FELLOW-CITIZENS OF TEXAS,

The enemy are upon us! A strong force surrounds the walls of San Antonio, and threaten that Garrison with the sword. Our country imperiously demands the service of every patriotic arm, and longer to continue in a state of *apathy* will be *criminal*. Citizens of Texas, descendants of Washington, awake! arouse yourselves!! The question is now to be decided, are we to continue as freemen, or bow beneath the rod of military despotism. Shall we, without a struggle, sacrifice our fortunes, our lives and our liberties, or shall we imitate the example of our forefathers, and hurl destruction upon the hands of our oppressors? The eyes of the world are upon us! All friends of liberty and of the rights of men, are anxious spectators of our conflict; or deeply enlisted in our cause. Shall we disappoint their hopes and expectations? No; let us at once fly to our arms, march to the battle field, meet the foe, and give renewed evidence to the world, that the arms of freemen, uplifted in defence of their rights and liberties, are irresistible. "Now is the day and now is the hour," that Texas expects every man to do his duty. Let us shew ourselves worthy to be free, *and we shall be free.* Our brethren of the United States have, with a generosity and a devotion to liberty, unparalleled in the annals of men, offered us every assistance. We have arms, ammunition, clothing and provisions; all we have to do, is to sustain ourselves for the present. Rest assured that

succors will reach us,' and that the people of the United States will not permit the chains of slavery to be rivetted on us.

Fellow-Citizens, your garrison at San Antonio is surrounded by more than twenty times their numbers. Will you see them perish by the hands of a mercenary soldiery, without an effort for their relief? They cannot sustain the seige more than thirty days; for the sake of humanity, before that time give them succor. Citizens of the east, your brethren of the Brazos and Colorado, expect your assistance, afford it, and check the march of the enemy and suffer not your own land to become the seat of war; without your immediate aid we cannot sustain the war. Fellow-citizens, I call upon you as your executive officer to "turn out;" it is your country that demands your help. He who longer slumbers on the volcano, must be a madman. He who refuses to aid his country in this, her hour of peril and danger is a traitor. All persons able to bear arms in Texas are called on to rendezvous at the town of Gonzales, with the least possible delay armed and equipped for battle. *Our rights and liberties must be protected*; to the battle field march and save the country. An approving world smiles upon us, the God of battles is on our side, and victory awaits us.

Confidently believing that your energies will be sufficient for the occasion, and that your efforts will be ultimately successful.

I subscribe myself your fellow-citizen,
HENRY SMITH,
Governor.

ABOVE, LEFT **Governor Henry Smith issued this broadside during the Alamo siege in an attempt to rouse stay-at-home Texians from their languor. Smith appealed to the colonists' American heritage when he reminded them that they were "descendants of Washington." Such rhetoric was habitual throughout the Texas rebellion. Even so, pleas such as this raised few recruits; it was a classic instance of too little, too late. (Courtesy of the Texas State Library and Archives Commission)**

ABOVE, RIGHT **While howitzer shells plummeted into the Alamo compound, Mexican gunners also directed solid shot against the walls. Round shot like this one appears to have been more effective. The constant pounding weakened the old walls to such a degree that the garrison had to shore up the north wall with a cribbing of horizontal logs supported by vertical braces. (Courtesy of the Houston Archeological Society)**

Perhaps, but the available guns were light field-pieces, not heavy siege cannon. Lacking heavier ordnance, the gunners had to position their light guns closer to the walls. They learned quickly, however, that venturing within 200 yards of the fort in daylight attracted the deadly Texian riflemen. Working throughout the night, therefore, the *Zapadores* began digging a series of entrenchments that zigzagged their way nearer to the old walls each night.

On 24 February, day two of the siege, Travis assumed full command when Bowie fell victim to a mysterious malady variously described as "hasty consumption" or "typhoid pneumonia". Whatever his illness, Bowie knew he was unable to command and instructed his volunteers to obey Travis.

That same day, Travis addressed an open letter to the "people of Texas and all Americans in the world." In it he recounted that the fort had "sustained a continual Bombardment and cannonade for 24 hours." He pledged that he would "never surrender or retreat" and swore "Victory or Death." The substance of the message, however, was an appeal for help. "I call on you in the name of Liberty," he entreated, "to come to our aid with all dispatch."

Yet, days dragged by and no help arrived. Travis knew that his couriers were getting through enemy lines. Why were the "people of Texas" ignoring him? The Texas government that should have been summoning and directing relief forces to the Alamo had ceased to exist. Where was General Houston? With the demise of the old government, he held no official authority. But Texians had scheduled a new convention to meet at Washington-on-the-Brazos to create a new government and declare independence from Mexico. Predictably, Houston rushed there to consolidate his power and secure his future. While Houston and the other Texian politicos quibbled, Santa Anna attacked. Travis and his men would have to fend as best they could.

On 1 March, 32 troops attached to Lieutenant George C. Kimbell's Gonzales ranging company cut their way through the enemy cordon and into the Alamo. Travis was grateful for any reinforcements, but knew he needed more than that paltry number. On 3 March he wrote the delegates at Washington-on-the-Brazos that he had lost faith in Colonel Fannin: "I look to the colonies alone for aid; unless it arrives soon, I shall have to fight the enemy on his own terms." He grew increasingly bitter that his fellow Texians seemed deaf to his constant appeals. "If my countrymen do not rally to my relief," he bemoaned, "I am determined to perish in the defense of this place, and my bones shall reproach my country for her neglect."

Travis's melancholy was wholly justified. The constant hammering by Mexican solid shot had weakened the walls. By day eleven of the siege, the *Zapadores* had established a battery within "musket shot" of the north wall. At that range, they did not require siege guns; each round bashed and battered until the wall was on the verge of collapse. Jameson directed work parties throughout the night, buttressing the wall with odd pieces of timber. But both he and Travis realized that this was only a stopgap measure. In the event of a determined assault, the north wall could not hold

On March 4, day 11 of the siege, Santa Anna called a council of war. He announced an assault for Sunday, 6 March. This bombshell stunned his officers. The Alamo's walls were crumbling; no Texian relief column had appeared; when provisions ran out, the garrison would have to surrender. There was simply no justification for a frontal assault on a stronghold bristling with cannon. Nevertheless, Santa Anna stubbornly insisted on storming the Alamo. But why?

The answer appeared to be the product of political, rather than military, considerations. Both Peña and Filisola recounted that Travis had

This daguerreotype, the earliest photograph of the Alamo church, surfaced in the 1990s. The photographer took the shot in the late 1840s before the US Army acquired the property in 1850 and added a roof and the famous parapet. At the time, one officer complained that the hump-shaped parapet gave the church the "appearance of the headboard of a bedstead." (Courtesy of the Prints and Photograph Collection, The Center for American History, University of Texas at Austin)

sent out an intermediary to discuss terms. Santa Anna rejoined that "they should surrender unconditionally, without guarantees, not even for life itself, since there should be no guarantees for traitors." Santa Anna tossed away his chance for a bloodless coup. "With this reply it is clear that all [Alamo defenders] were determined to lose their existence," Filisola remonstrated, "selling it as dearly as possible." Peña speculated that the dictator triggered the assault to prevent the garrison's surrender. Santa Anna the politician needed a glorious victory, not a dreary capitulation. As Peña explained it, the generalissimo "would have regretted taking the Alamo without clamor and without bloodshed, for some believe that without these there is no glory."

Captain Fernando Urissa recalled Santa Anna's disregard for the lives of his soldiers. He told how General Manuel Fernandez Castrillón insisted that a frontal assault was in violation of all accepted custom and would surely result in the needless loss of many *soldados*. At his dinner, the generalissimo flourished a chicken leg to bolster his argument: *What are the lives of soldiers than so many chickens? I tell you, the Alamo must fall, and my orders must be obeyed at all hazards. If our soldiers are driven back, the next line in their rear must force those before them forward, and compel them to scale the walls, cost what it may.* With that, all opposition crumbled; it was obvious that His Excellency had already made his decision.

The attack order of 5 March scheduled the onslaught for five o'clock the following morning. The Mexican cannon fell silent toward the end of the day. Santa Anna hoped that weary rebels would take advantage of the lull to catch up on their sleep. If his *soldados* approached silently under the cover of darkness, they might be over the walls before the bleary-eyed defenders reached their posts.

The plan worked. For twelve days Alamo defenders had endured almost constant bombardment. Now, near the end of their tether, they collapsed in exhausted heaps. Travis posted a few picket guards, but they too seemed to have nodded off. All was silent inside the compound as the stroke of midnight proclaimed the beginning of day 13 of the siege – 6 March 1836.

ASSAULT

Conversely, that hour saw the Mexican camp come alive. Officers and NCOs inspected their men. *Zapadores* issued ladders and crowbars; sergeants saw that *soldados* fastened their shako straps; officers made certain that all assault troops wore their issue brogans. Lastly, they scrutinized weapons. Santa Anna's order had been ominous: "The arms, principally the bayonets, should be in perfect order."

By 3.00am all were ready. The pre-dawn hours were cold and many troops stood shivering in place for hours. Column commanders

Cazador, Toluca Battalion. José Enrique de la Peña recalled that a "single cannon volley" swept away half the *cazadores* (light infantrymen) in one company of the Toluca Battalion. This poor fellow is one of the unfortunate *cazadores* caught in that "horrible fire." (Gary Zaboly, illustrator, from *Texian Iliad*. Author's Collection)

informed His Excellency that the troops were losing their edge. Finally at 5.30, he signaled the advance.

All proceeded smoothly as the columns pressed forward under a vivid moon. Massed columns provided outstanding targets, but Santa Anna needed the steady veterans to box in faltering recruits. He had assembled some 1,700 veteran infantrymen for the assault, but had excused his newest recruits. General Cos, commanding 200 *fusileros* and *cazadores* of the Aldama Battalion and 100 *fusileros* of the San Luis militia, marched toward the northwest corner of the fort. Colonel Francisco Duque, at the head of 395, drove hard against the north wall. He had under his command six *fusilero* and one *cazador* companies from the Toluca Battalion along with three *fusilero* companies detached from the San Luis Battalion. Colonel José María Romero approached the Alamo from the east with some 300 *fusileros* of the Matamoros and Jimenez battalions. Colonel Juan Morales led three companies of *cazadores* – about 100 men detached from the Matamoros, Jimenez, and San Luis battalions – toward the low parapet by the church.

Santa Anna directed General Ramírez y Sesma to post 369 cavalrymen along the perimeter of the battlefield to "scout the country" and "prevent the possibility of escape." He assembled these horsemen from the Dolores Regiment, Vera Cruz Platoon, Coahuila Company, and the Rio Grande Presidial Company.

As the Mexican columns moved within range, all remained quiet inside the Alamo. But the silence itself was nerve-wracking. The tension finally became more than one anonymous *soldado* could bear. "*Viva Santa Anna!*" he bellowed. "*Viva la Republica!*" screamed another. Then, hundreds of voices shattered the stillness. Watching from his command post, Santa Anna flew into a rage. He later lambasted these "imprudent huzzas" for awaking the "sleeping vigilance of the defenders."

The racket did alert the defenders. Groggy, they roused themselves and scurried to their posts. Travis sprang from his cot, grabbed his shotgun, and rushed to his north wall battery. "Come on, boys, the Mexicans are upon us," he shouted, "and we'll give them Hell!"

Travis commanded a battery of 8-pdrs that covered the approaches to the north wall. It is possible that he operated the gun pictured here. There is no way of knowing, of course, but residents of San Antonio discovered this eight-pound tube (along with others of like caliber) following the battle. The cannon remains on the grounds of the Alamo today. (Photo by Deborah Bloys Hardin, Author's Collection)

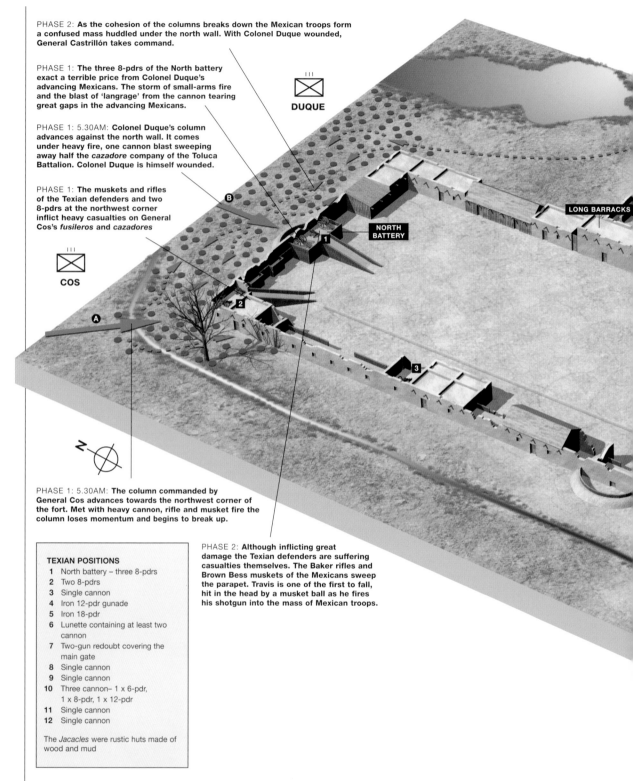

PHASE 2: **As the cohesion of the columns breaks down the Mexican troops form a confused mass huddled under the north wall. With Colonel Duque wounded, General Castrillón takes command.**

PHASE 1: **The three 8-pdrs of the North battery exact a terrible price from Colonel Duque's advancing Mexicans. The storm of small-arms fire and the blast of 'langrage' from the cannon tearing great gaps in the advancing Mexicans.**

PHASE 1: 5.30AM: **Colonel Duque's column advances against the north wall. It comes under heavy fire, one cannon blast sweeping away half the *cazadore* company of the Toluca Battalion. Colonel Duque is himself wounded.**

PHASE 1: **The muskets and rifles of the Texian defenders and two 8-pdrs at the northwest corner inflict heavy casualties on General Cos's *fusileros* and *cazadores***

DUQUE

COS

NORTH BATTERY

LONG BARRACKS

PHASE 1: 5.30AM: **The column commanded by General Cos advances towards the northwest corner of the fort. Met with heavy cannon, rifle and musket fire the column loses momentum and begins to break up.**

PHASE 2: **Although inflicting great damage the Texian defenders are suffering casualties themselves. The Baker rifles and Brown Bess muskets of the Mexicans sweep the parapet. Travis is one of the first to fall, hit in the head by a musket ball as he fires his shotgun into the mass of Mexican troops.**

TEXIAN POSITIONS

1   North battery – three 8-pdrs
2   Two 8-pdrs
3   Single cannon
4   Iron 12-pdr gunade
5   Iron 18-pdr
6   Lunette containing at least two cannon
7   Two-gun redoubt covering the main gate
8   Single cannon
9   Single cannon
10 Three cannon– 1 x 6-pdr, 1 x 8-pdr, 1 x 12-pdr
11 Single cannon
12 Single cannon

The *Jacacles* were rustic huts made of wood and mud

THE ALAMO, 6 MARCH 1836

Viewed from the west showing the initial Mexican attacks which, savaged by the fort's cannon and small-arms fire, break down in disorder.

PHASE 1: 5.30AM: **Colonel Romero's column advances against the east wall. Swept by canister shot from the cannon atop the church as well as small-arms fire it veers to the right.**

ROMERO

PHASE 1: **Texian defenders and the cannon atop the church and along the east wall sweep Colonel Romero's advancing column with heavy fire.**

Alamo
Garrison

TRAVIS

PHASE 1: 5.30AM: **Colonel Morales' column of light infantry advances on the low parapet running between the church and the buildings around the main gate. This is supposedly the fort's weak spot, but protected by the abatis and manned by Crockett's rifle-armed Tennesseans this is far from the truth. Taking casualties Morales men seek shelter behind the *jacales* at the southwest corner of the fort.**

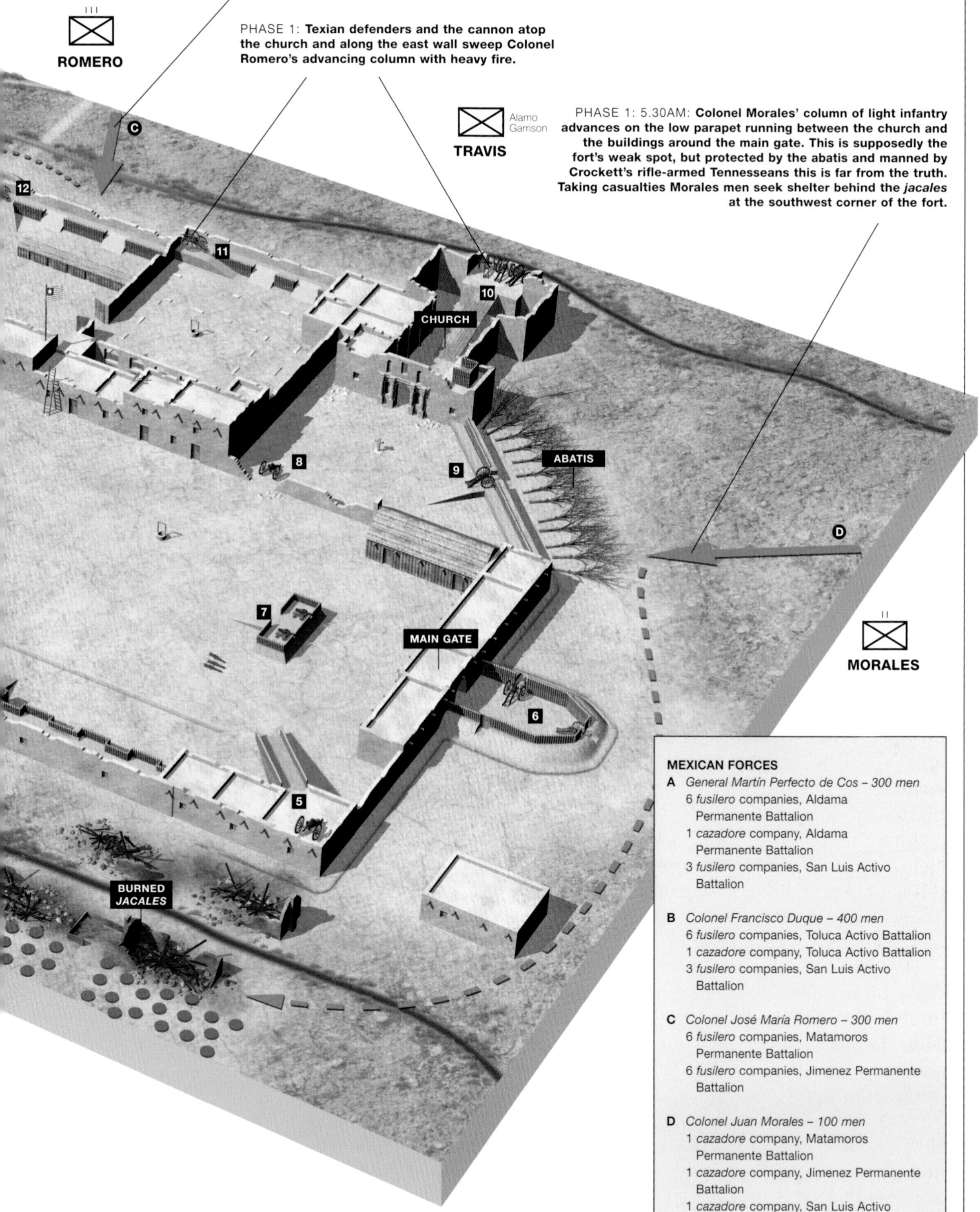

12

11

10

CHURCH

C

8

9

ABATIS

D

7

MAIN GATE

MORALES

6

5

**BURNED
JACALES**

MEXICAN FORCES

A *General Martín Perfecto de Cos – 300 men*
6 *fusilero* companies, Aldama
Permanente Battalion
1 *cazadore* company, Aldama
Permanente Battalion
3 *fusilero* companies, San Luis Activo
Battalion

B *Colonel Francisco Duque – 400 men*
6 *fusilero* companies, Toluca Activo Battalion
1 *cazadore* company, Toluca Activo Battalion
3 *fusilero* companies, San Luis Activo
Battalion

C *Colonel José María Romero – 300 men*
6 *fusilero* companies, Matamoros
Permanente Battalion
6 *fusilero* companies, Jimenez Permanente
Battalion

D *Colonel Juan Morales – 100 men*
1 *cazadore* company, Matamoros
Permanente Battalion
1 *cazadore* company, Jimenez Permanente
Battalion
1 *cazadore* company, San Luis Activo
Battalion

39

Gunners ran to their cannon. They had crammed their pieces with langrage: bits of horseshoes, links of chain, nails, sections of door hinges; indeed, any trace of rusty scrap they could scrounge. Packing that lethal charge, the artillery doubled as giant shotguns. Bathed in bright moonlight, the enemy columns appeared in their sights. A gust of metallic wreckage swept the columns like a "terrible shower." Peña watched with revulsion as a blast from a single cannon swept off half the company of Toluca *cazadores*. Another *soldado* recalled that he and his comrades suffered the results of "horrible fire."

The packed bodies soaked up the force of the scatter shot, jagged shards slammed home, gashed as they plowed through the ranks, and finally stopped … lodged in their victims. Eight-pound balls smashed bodies, spraying bone fragments that themselves wounded and even killed men. Billowing smoke and the mass of men in front of them blinded those trapped deep inside the throng, but they could still hear the bedlam: the tormented screams of mangled comrades.

But the assault troops were returning fire. Alamo riflemen had to reveal themselves above the parapet to snipe at the enemy below. One Mexican recalled that those atop the wall "could not remain for a single second without being killed." Travis had just unloaded both barrels of his shotgun into Duque's column when a slug slammed through his forehead and into his brain. Santa Anna might have been able to smash down the "door" to Texas, but William Barret Travis never surrendered the "key".

Disorder

The devastating fire savaged Mexican ranks. It ripped columns asunder, but still they drove forward. In response to the murderous fire, Cos shifted his forces against the west wall. As unit integrity broke down, however, many swept around the corner and swirled together with Duque's men huddled at the base of the north wall. A painful leg wound dropped Colonel Duque. In their headlong dash, his men trampled him. Just as he was about to perish under their feet, more attentive *soldados* plucked him from the press of grinding brogans. As they helped the addled Duque off the field, General Castrillón took command of the column. Angling in from the east, Romero's troops found themselves facing direct cannon fire coming from the rear of the church. To avoid this lethal welter, Romero ordered a right oblique toward the north wall. There, it ran into the intermingled mob of Cos and Duque. Romero's men joined the jumbled horde, only increasing the bedlam.

Along the south wall, Morales's column was faring no better. He drove his *cazadores* hard against the wooden palisade, but ran headlong into a sturdy abatis, lethal canister rounds, and Crockett's riflemen. Thus, Morales led his men along the south wall toward the southwest corner and the 18-pdr. Once there, they were able to take cover behind the ruins of small houses.

Back along the north wall, Mexican assault troops faced a stark choice. Those who had pressed themselves flush against the wall were under the guns. There, they were relatively safe from enemy fire. Knowing that, other *soldados* who remained in the open pushed forward hoping to share this haven. There were, however, too many bodies and too little space. In their panic, the stronger and larger shoved aside the

American illustrator Gary S. Zaboly depicts the fighting inside the Alamo compound. Mexican assault troops pour into the fort, while defenders abandon the walls and retreat into the long barracks and the church. One resolute Texian, however, refuses to forsake his wounded comrade and faces the onslaught of elite *cazadores*. (From *Texian Iliad*. Author's Collection)

OVERLEAF

THE DEATH OF WILLIAM BARRET TRAVIS

Thanks to his servant Joe, we know many details surrounding Travis's demise. Joe's slave status spared him the fate of the other Alamo defenders. Although illiterate, at least three contemporaries recorded his account. According to Joe: Travis "seeing the enemy under the mouths of the cannon with scaling ladders, discharged his double barreled gun down upon them." Brown Bess muskets and Baker Rifles replied in kind. A slug took Travis in the head; he tumbled down the earthen ramp of the north wall battery, his shotgun "falling upon the enemy." With his master down and dying, Joe "ensconced himself in a house" along the west wall. A Mexican officer found him there and offered safe conduct. Later Joe escaped to tell his tale. Travis vowed he would "never surrender or retreat." He proved as good as his word. What Churchill said of Harold Godwinson applies equally to Travis: "unconquerable except by death, which does not count in honour." (Angus McBride)

smaller and weaker. Yet others continued to thrust ahead. It became a cruel choice – to be shot by the rebels or smothered by comrades.

The final option was to scale the wall and kill their tormenters. Back at his command post, Santa Anna influenced that decision. Watching the attack bog down along the north wall, he ordered in his reserves – the elite *Zapadores*. Driving within range, they unleashed a volley toward the few defenders still atop the north wall. Most of their rounds, however, fell short, wounding and killing their comrades huddled below. "Thus it was," Filisola grumbled, "that most of our dead and wounded … were caused by this misfortune." He believed "not a fourth of them were the result of enemy fire." His percentages may have been exaggerated, but far too many *soldados* fell to Mexican bullets. This "friendly fire" gave the huddled mass the impetus to scale the wall, but they needed someone to lead them. The attack was faltering.

Breakthrough

General Juan Amador began the grueling 12-foot ascent and called on the *soldados* to follow his example. All ladders had gone missing, but Jameson's improvised repairs had left numerous gaps and toeholds. Amador's audacity shamed the attackers to action. Ultimately, despair and sheer weight of numbers replaced all of Santa Anna's

Mexican Light Cavalryman. Santa Anna placed troopers such as these outside the walls of the Alamo to ride down any rebel defender who sought escape. They performed that duty with lethal effectiveness. (Gary Zaboly, illustrator, from *Texian Iliad*. Author's Collection).

careful preparation. This swarm retained no semblance of organization. Unit integrity broke down. Commands went unheard and unheeded. Even so, each *soldado* knew what he must do: scale the wall and perhaps survive, or perish where he crouched.

So they climbed. To reach the enemy, they had to heave and elbow a path over their friends. Amador grappled up and over the parapet and fell into the courtyard below. His men dropped in behind him. For now – regardless to what units they belonged – they were his men. Amador and the first men inside the fort located a small postern and swung it open. Their comrades flooded through. From that moment, the outcome of the assault was beyond doubt.

Occasionally when a battle hangs in the balance, an individual tips the scales toward victory. History provides numerous instances – Desaix at Marengo, Macdonnell at Hougoumont, Chamberlain on Little Round Top. At the Alamo, that man was Juan Amador.

The only portions of the 1836 Alamo compound that remain are the church and the lower floor of the long barracks. Here one can see the long barracks as it appears today. This view looks toward what would have been the north wall during the battle. Inside the rooms of the long barracks much of the fiercest fighting took place. (Photo by Deborah Bloys Hardin, Author's Collection)

The defenders abandoned the north wall – after that, events unfolded quickly. At the southwest corner Morales's *cazadores* picked off the gunners manning the 18-pdr, scaled the wall, and poured into the compound. Some defiant *norteamericanos* endeavored to make a stand in the open plaza, but found themselves caught between the fire of Morales's troops streaming in from the south and that of Amador's men flooding in from the north. The defenders fell back into the long barracks. Crockett and his riflemen took cover inside the church.

Others, however, concluded that the Alamo had become a deathtrap. As many as 75 darted over the wall and sought cover in the chaparral outside. Santa Anna had anticipated their dash for safety and had positioned Ramírez y Sesma's lancers to intercept it. In his after-battle report Ramírez y Sesma noted the "desperate resistance" of the fugitives. He twice had to dispatch reinforcements before his horsemen eradicated these rebels who were "ready to sell their lives at a very high price." But soon the job was done. All had died on the points of vicious lances. All, that is, save one. A lone defender dug so far into the underbrush that the lancers could not root him out. Hence, they shot him where he squatted.

Last Resistance

Inside the fort, the defenders prepared to make their final stand. The Texians had abandoned the outer perimeter in such haste that they had neglected to spike their guns. Now the Mexicans hauled them into the courtyard and methodically blasted each door into the long barracks. *Soldados* tore through the shattered entryways to finish the work begun by the captured cannon. There in the darkness, adversaries grappled with bayonet and butcher knife. Breaking into a room along the south wall, Morales's men discovered one rebel too faint and delirious to rise from his sick bed. By that point, the *soldados* were beyond pity: they killed him where he lay. But then, pity was never a sentiment Jim Bowie had especially valued.

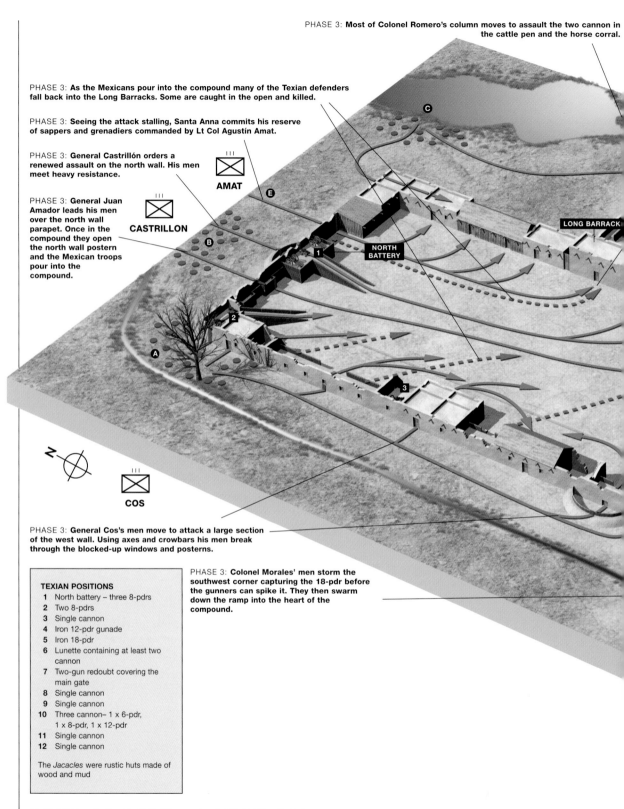

PHASE 3: Most of Colonel Romero's column moves to assault the two cannon in the cattle pen and the horse corral.

PHASE 3: As the Mexicans pour into the compound many of the Texian defenders fall back into the Long Barracks. Some are caught in the open and killed.

PHASE 3: Seeing the attack stalling, Santa Anna commits his reserve of sappers and grenadiers commanded by Lt Col Agustín Amat.

PHASE 3: General Castrillón orders a renewed assault on the north wall. His men meet heavy resistance.

AMAT

PHASE 3: General Juan Amador leads his men over the north wall parapet. Once in the compound they open the north wall postern and the Mexican troops pour into the compound.

CASTRILLON

NORTH BATTERY

LONG BARRACK

COS

PHASE 3: General Cos's men move to attack a large section of the west wall. Using axes and crowbars his men break through the blocked-up windows and posterns.

PHASE 3: Colonel Morales' men storm the southwest corner capturing the 18-pdr before the gunners can spike it. They then swarm down the ramp into the heart of the compound.

TEXIAN POSITIONS
1 North battery – three 8-pdrs
2 Two 8-pdrs
3 Single cannon
4 Iron 12-pdr gunade
5 Iron 18-pdr
6 Lunette containing at least two cannon
7 Two-gun redoubt covering the main gate
8 Single cannon
9 Single cannon
10 Three cannon– 1 x 6-pdr, 1 x 8-pdr, 1 x 12-pdr
11 Single cannon
12 Single cannon

The *Jacales* were rustic huts made of wood and mud

THE ALAMO, 6 MARCH 1836
Viewed from the west showing the final Mexican assault and the storming of the compound.

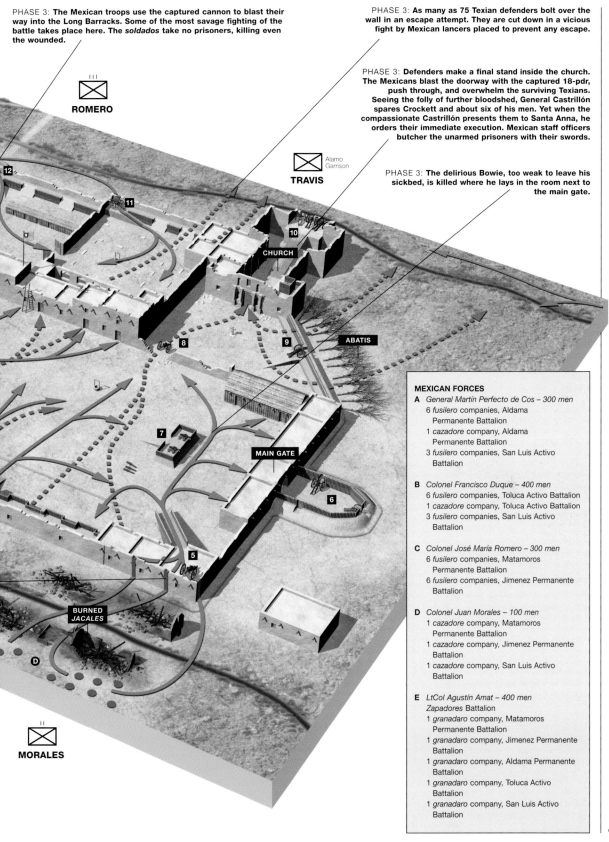

PHASE 3: **The Mexican troops use the captured cannon to blast their way into the Long Barracks. Some of the most savage fighting of the battle takes place here. The** *soldados* **take no prisoners, killing even the wounded.**

PHASE 3: **As many as 75 Texian defenders bolt over the wall in an escape attempt. They are cut down in a vicious fight by Mexican lancers placed to prevent any escape.**

PHASE 3: **Defenders make a final stand inside the church. The Mexicans blast the doorway with the captured 18-pdr, push through, and overwhelm the surviving Texians. Seeing the folly of further bloodshed, General Castrillón spares Crockett and about six of his men. Yet when the compassionate Castrillón presents them to Santa Anna, he orders their immediate execution. Mexican staff officers butcher the unarmed prisoners with their swords.**

PHASE 3: **The delirious Bowie, too weak to leave his sickbed, is killed where he lays in the room next to the main gate.**

ROMERO

Alamo Garrison
TRAVIS

12

11

10

CHURCH

8

9

ABATIS

7

MAIN GATE

6

5

BURNED JACALES

D

MORALES

MEXICAN FORCES

A *General Martín Perfecto de Cos – 300 men*
6 *fusilero* companies, Aldama Permanente Battalion
1 *cazadore* company, Aldama Permanente Battalion
3 *fusilero* companies, San Luis Activo Battalion

B *Colonel Francisco Duque – 400 men*
6 *fusilero* companies, Toluca Activo Battalion
1 *cazadore* company, Toluca Activo Battalion
3 *fusilero* companies, San Luis Activo Battalion

C *Colonel José María Romero – 300 men*
6 *fusilero* companies, Matamoros Permanente Battalion
6 *fusilero* companies, Jimenez Permanente Battalion

D *Colonel Juan Morales – 100 men*
1 *cazadore* company, Matamoros Permanente Battalion
1 *cazadore* company, Jimenez Permanente Battalion
1 *cazadore* company, San Luis Activo Battalion

E *LtCol Agustín Amat – 400 men*
Zapadores Battalion
1 *granadaro* company, Matamoros Permanente Battalion
1 *granadaro* company, Jimenez Permanente Battalion
1 *granadaro* company, Aldama Permanente Battalion
1 *granadaro* company, Toluca Activo Battalion
1 *granadaro* company, San Luis Activo Battalion

The Alamo church was the last to fall. Employing the massive 18-pdr, the *centralistas* knocked aside the sandbags blocking the main door and rammed through. All but six or seven of the defenders were overwhelmed and slaughtered. The battle was won – there was no need for senseless bloodshed. General Castrillón intervened and ordered his *soldados* to spare these defenseless adversaries.

Aftermath

With the battle over, Santa Anna entered the fort. As he assessed the carnage, Castrillón presented his prisoners. He urged humane treatment for these hapless individuals, but His Excellency countered with a "gesture of indignation" and ordered their immediate execution. Not all Mexicans countenanced such barbarity. Urissa noted that "Castrillón turned aside with tears in his eyes, and my heart was too full to speak."

That bloody deed still provokes controversy among students of the battle. Peña minced no words when he reported that Crockett numbered among those prisoners. Still, many refuse to accept that the "Lion of the West" could have died any other way but in the thick of battle, surrounded by heaps of enemy slain. In truth, none of the evidence is beyond question. As befits a legend, Crockett's death remains clouded in myth and mystery. Perhaps the most candid assumption came from a Texas visitor in 1837. "That Crockett fell at the Alamo is all that is known," he reported, "by whom or how, no one can tell."

Finally, it matters far more where Crockett died than how. Like all the defenders, he joined the garrison to fight for republican institutions and against centralist tyranny. They were never zealots bent on ritual suicide. Such fanaticism was no part of their cultural tradition. They were soldiers – citizen soldiers who willingly placed themselves in harm's way for kith and kin. True, they may have been willing to die for cause and country, but that was never their aspiration. They fervently hoped such a sacrifice would prove unnecessary.

Despite all the "Victory or Death" hyperbole, Travis never stopped calling on the government for reinforcements. Torn by discord, the provisional government could not deliver on its pledge to provide relief, and the men of the Alamo paid the price of that dereliction. To a man they followed their orders; to a man they stood firm against overwhelming odds; to a man they fell. That should qualify them as heroes by any reasonable criterion.

What the dawn revealed was surreal in its terror. Peña noted the "unbearable and nauseating" stench. But he described the sights as well as the smells: *The bodies, with their blackened and bloody faces disfigured by desperate death, their hair and uniforms burning at once, presented a dreadful and truly hellish sight. Quite soon the bodies were left naked by the fire, others by*

ABOVE **Private, New Orleans Greys. After evacuating the walls, Alamo defenders fell back into the long barracks. The Mexicans blasted through the barricaded doorways with the fort's cannon. The remaining Texians were trapped inside. This terrified volunteer well knows that any surrender attempt would be fruitless; foreign rebels can expect no mercy. (Gary Zaboly, illustrator, from *Texian Iliad.* Author's Collection)**

OPPOSITE **The azure standard of the First Company of Texan Volunteers from New Orleans, better known as the New Orleans Greys. Frequently misidentified as the Alamo garrison flag, it was merely one of many the Mexicans captured there. Following the battle, Santa Anna dispatched the standard to Mexico City, where it remains today. (Courtesy of the Texas State Library and Archives Commission)**

disgraceful rapacity, especially among our men. The enemy could be identified by their whiteness, by their robust and bulky shapes. What a sad spectacle, that of the dead and dying! What a horror, to inspect the area and find the remains of friends!

This "sad spectacle" seems to have left Santa Anna unmoved. Captain Urissa observed him strolling among the smoldering corpses. Pointing at the dead, Santa Anna betrayed no emotion whatsoever. "Urissa, these are the chickens," he remarked. "Much blood has been shed, but the battle is over; it was but a small affair."

Earlier writers have derided Santa Anna for the callousness of that remark, but in purely military terms he was correct. Historians still debate the exact number of Alamo slain. Currently, the names of 189 defenders appear on the official list, but ongoing research may increase the final tally to as many as 257. Much discussion also surrounds the number of Mexican casualties. If one considers those who died of their wounds in the weeks and months following the battle, the number of Mexican dead may have reached as many as 600. By way of comparison, Wellington suffered more casualties (some 5,365) at Talavera than the total number of combatants at the Alamo. So judging simply by the numbers, it was a "small affair."

But numbers alone can never convey the real meaning of the Alamo. Travis had foretold that his very bones would rebuke the Texians, and now his sacrifice and that of his comrades had a powerful effect. The slaughter at the Alamo finally awakened the Texians to their peril. It forcefully drove home that the war was far from over and they must unite or lose all. The Alamo and its defenders quickly transcended mere history, entering the realm of myth. Ironically, if Santa Anna had been willing to take prisoners he would have deprived the battle of its moral power. Instead, he insisted on killing the defenders to the last man; then he tossed their naked corpses on a pyre and burned them like so much

This woodcut from the *Crockett Almanac* is typical of the many popular culture depictions that sprang up following the Alamo battle. Here, Davy joyfully bashes a Mexican officer with his clubbed rifle. Reared on images such as this, many Americans found it difficult to believe that their hero might not have died fighting to the last. (Author's collection)

OVERLEAF

DAVID CROCKETT AND HIS TENNESSEANS FALL BACK INTO THE ALAMO CHURCH
Most accounts have Crockett defending the palisade between the church and south wall. As Mexican troops poured into the compound they promptly out-flanked Crockett's position. Thus, he prudently had his men take cover inside the church. While Crockett occasionally affected frontier garb to sustain his political persona, he actually favored more conventional clothing. One Texas lady stressed that he dressed "like a gentleman and not a backwoodsman"; a Mexican sergeant recalled Crockett wore "a coat with capes to it"; General Cos remembered him as "well-dressed." Nonetheless, Susanna Dickinson viewed Crockett's corpse and noted his "peculiar cap by his side." So, notwithstanding his urbane apparel, he does appear to have sported a coonskin cap! Crockett died a national hero ... and a certifiable eccentric. (Angus McBride)

The Texian Star and Stripes Flag. In his letter of 24 February, Travis wrote that he had answered Santa Anna's surrender demands with a cannon shot and "our flag still waves proudly from the walls." But to which flag did Travis refer? Recent scholarship strongly suggests that it was this flag, which was at the time the de facto national flag of Texas. (Photo by Deborah Bloys Hardin, Author's Collection)

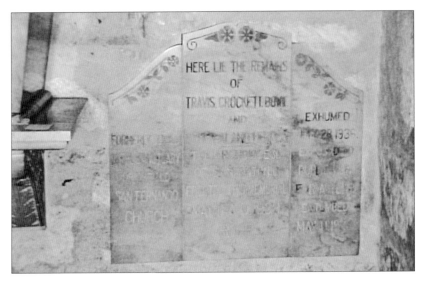

LEFT Alamo courier Juan Seguín located the site of the funeral pyres and claimed to have collected the remains of the defenders in an urn that he buried in a corner of the San Fernando church. During the 1936 restoration of the church, workers uncovered charred bones and bits of cloth. Subsequently, church officials placed them in this crypt. Nevertheless, many scholars doubt that the remains are actually those of the Alamo's defenders. (Photo by Deborah Bloys Hardin, Author's Collection)

rubbish. Like Leonidas at Thermopylae and Roland at Roncesvalles, the fall of Travis and his men provided a potent rallying symbol, filling Texians with righteous anger. Less than three weeks after the battle, a Texas newspaper paid homage to the men of the Alamo:

Spirits of the mighty, though fallen! Honors and rest are with ye: the spark of immortality which animated your forms, shall brighten into a flame, and Texas, the whole world, shall hail ye like the demi-Gods of old, as founders of new actions and as patterns of imitation!

Six weeks later on the boggy field of San Jacinto, Santa Anna would feel the heat of that flame.

URREA'S ADVANCE

Santa Anna fancied himself the "Napoleon of the West," but General José Urrea came closer to earning that title. Like the French emperor, he seized the momentum and never relinquished it. Santa Anna had heard rumors of the Texians' Matamoros Expedition and dispatched Urrea to secure that vital port. Arriving there on 31 January, he discovered that Matamoros was under no threat of attack; Grant and Johnson remained 150 miles to the north, still trying to drum up support for their harebrained scheme. The speed and suddenness of Urrea's advance was reminiscent of Bonaparte's 1805 encirclement of Ulm or his 1815 drive on Charleroi. Lamentably for the Texians, rebel commanders performed more like General Mack than the Iron Duke.

On 17 February Urrea drove across the Rio Grande. His spies had informed him that Johnson and Grant had assembled their forces in and around the village of San Patricio. No longer would Urrea sit idle; he drove rapidly northward to the Nueces River to strike before the rebels could shake off their lethargy. Urrea rode at the head of 320 infantry, 230 dragoons, and a 4-pdr field gun. He left behind about 200 *soldados* in Matamoros. They would follow later, but now speed was essential and he could move faster with fewer men.

On the night of 25 February, Urrea's men received their first taste of the freakish Texas winter. Notwithstanding the "cold and penetrating" north winds, Urrea dared not break pace. All his *soldados* suffered, but those from Yucatán most of all. Most were Mayan Indians used to the climes of their steamy peninsula. Urrea noted that "six soldiers of the battalion of Yucatán died from exposure to the cold." The following day brought icy rain and even more misery. "The night was very raw and excessively cold," Urrea lamented.

Their sacrifice was about to pay off. Blithely unaware of Urrea's proximity, Grant and a detachment were out rounding up wild mustangs, leaving Johnson in San Patricio with about 60 men. At 3.00am on 27 February, Urrea struck using the bucketing rain as cover. The Mexicans fell upon Johnson's men with such swiftness and surprise that they never had an opportunity to rally. By dawn, Urrea had captured nearby Fort Lipantitlán and secured the town; his men had killed 20 rebels and captured another 32. Only eight, including Colonel Johnson, managed to escape. Urrea lost one man killed and four wounded.

In San Patricio, Urrea received intelligence that Grant was returning from his horse-hunting foray with between 40 and 50 "picked riflemen." Urrea feared what riflemen could do if they had the opportunity to seek cover and so resolved to deny them the opportunity. He led 80 dragoons to a mott about 25 miles southwest of San Patricio. He knew that Grant's party must travel along the trail that passed through the coppice that locals called Los Cuates de Agua Dulce. "I divided my force into six groups," Urrea explained, "and hid them in the woods."

On the morning of 2 March, Grant and his party rode into Urrea's trap. The action unfolded as if Urrea had scripted it himself. Indeed, his diary entry seemed almost lackadaisical:

> *Between ten and eleven in the morning Dr. Grant arrived. He was attacked and vanquished by the parties under my command and that of Colonel Francisco Garay. Dr. Grant and forty of the riflemen were left dead on the field and we took six prisoners besides their arms, munitions, and horses.*

Urrea recorded no casualties. Now that he had brushed aside Johnson and Grant, Urrea directed his attention toward his primary objective: Fannin and his Goliad garrison.

At Goliad, Fannin was attempting to consolidate his forces. On 11 March he had dispatched Amon B. King's company to evacuate some stranded Texian families in Refugio. But instead of removing the families as ordered, King took it upon himself to terrorize loyalist *rancheros*. Whilst doing so, he and his men stumbled onto one of Urrea's advance cavalry detachments. The Mexican horsemen withdrew following a brief skirmish. King should have taken the opportunity to retire to Goliad with the noncombatants. Yet, he dispatched a courier to Fannin requesting reinforcements. Fannin foolishly hastened William Ward's Georgia Battalion to assist King. This was only the first of Fannin's many appalling command decisions.

Ward arrived in Refugio on 13 March. King and his men had fallen back to the old Refugio Mission and were skirmishing with about 60 of Urrea's vanguard troops. Once the Georgia Battalion arrived on the field, the Mexicans retired. Fate had handed the Texians another chance to vacate Refugio – and, once again, they squandered it. If Ward and King had immediately retreated toward Goliad, they might have forestalled their ruin. Contrary to all logic, however, they lingered to attack a group of local Tejanos. His cavalry vanguard had returned to inform Urrea that a small rebel force occupied Refugio. He ordered Captain Rafael Pretalia's company of dragoons to gallop toward the town and engage whatever force he encountered. Urrea, of course, did not expect Pretalia's cavalry to defeat Ward and King, he only wanted to pin them down until he could bring up the bulk of his infantry.

At dawn on 14 March Urrea arrived with his main force. According to plan, he found Pretalia skirmishing with Ward's Georgians, who had holed up in the old mission. Urrea recorded that the Texians "opened up a lively fire," but that was their undoing. King and Ward had not brought sufficient ammunition for a daylong encounter. By nightfall both units were dangerously short of powder and ball. Greatly out-numbered and short of bullets, Ward and King sought to escape under the cover of darkness.

Unfamiliar with the countryside and on foot on the sweeping prairies, the Texian fugitives never stood a chance. Urrea unleashed vengeful *rancheros*, who soon tracked them down. Mexican tories rounded up King's men and dragged them back to Refugio, where, on 16 March, Urrea ordered them to be shot. Given his subsequent kindness toward Texian prisoners of war, Urrea's summary execution of King's men seems curious. No doubt Urrea had learned about King's terror campaign against Tejano civilians, reports which did not put him in a forgiving mood. On the verge of starvation, Ward's men wandered on the prairies for days, before they too were captured. Back in Goliad, Fannin vainly awaited the return of King and Ward.

Urrea had performed superbly. He had attacked swiftly, achieved surprise, and continually kept the rebels off balance. He had negated the Texians' strengths – their courage and their rifles – and exploited their weakness – foolhardiness and ineptitude. Because his opposition was so clumsy, historians have never awarded Urrea the recognition he deserved. The general extolled his men, but was never one to boast of his own achievements. As he prepared to attack Goliad, Urrea could only pray that Colonel Fannin would prove as incompetent as his previous opponents.

A portrait purported to be that of James Walker Fannin, Jr. Some have attributed the canvas to Samuel F.B. Morse, originator of the Morse code. Several features, however, appear anachronistic. In 1836 Fannin would not have worn a uniform such as the one depicted here – or any uniform at all. Eyewitness accounts have him clad in civilian attire: specifically, an overcoat made of "India rubber". (Courtesy of the Dallas Historical Society)

This photograph shows the northwest bastion of the Presidio La Bahía as it appears today. In the background is the presidio's chapel, where the Mexicans confined the Texian prisoners prior to their execution. The early drawings and photographs of the chapel prior to reconstruction do not show the bell tower. Many now believe that it was not present during the 1836 campaign. (Photo by Deborah Bloys Hardin. Author's Collection)

THE BATTLE OF COLETO CREEK

For the historian attempting to fathom his behavior, **James Walker Fannin, Jr.**, remains an enigma. He was Dr. Isham Fannin's son, but while still a boy he was adopted by James W. Walker, his maternal grandfather. The lad consequently appears to have suffered an identity crisis. In 1819 he entered the United States Military Academy under the name James F. Walker. His time there was shortlived, however, and he withdrew in 1821. Returning to his native Georgia he tried his hand at planting. He married Minerva Fort and the couple had two daughters. While happy in his family life, his business affairs failed. In 1834, Fannin – who had once more assumed his real name – moved his family to Mexican Texas. Fannin and his young family settled in the port settlement of Velasco, where he immediately became embroiled with the War Party. He enjoyed putting on the airs of a successful planter, but he made what little money he had as a slave trader.

Fannin became a vocal critic of the centralist government and when fighting erupted he was present, rifle in hand, at the battle of Gonzales. On 28 October 1835, he made a name for himself when he and Jim Bowie led the Texian rebels to victory at the battle of Concepción. Fannin was a Houston crony, and on 7 December the general commissioned him as a colonel in the then non-existent regular army. An agent of the provisional government, he recruited volunteers for the ill-fated Matamoros Expedition. At this juncture Fannin's ambition and his penchant to play politics merged. Because of his association with Governor Smith, the Council mistrusted Houston. Knowing that the volunteers would never accept his leadership, Houston withdrew his support for the expedition. Suddenly, Houston was out of favor and Fannin found himself the darling of the Council. On 7 February 1836, the Provisional Regiment of Volunteers at Goliad elected Fannin its colonel. From 12 February to 12 March, he also acted as commander-in-chief of the regular army. Unperturbed by the incongruous nature of his dual command, Fannin served as the colonel of a regiment of volunteers while at the same time acting as commander of an army of phantom regulars. But then,

His unwillingness to abandon his guns greatly hampered Fannin's withdrawal from Goliad. The cannon depicted here is one of those that he carried with him and employed at the Battle of Coleto Creek. Note the missing cascabel and trunnions. Following San Jacinto, the retreating Mexicans disabled the tube to prevent its future use by the Texians. (Photo by Deborah Bloys Hardin, Author's Collection)

A stone obelisk is the major feature of the Fannin Battleground State Historical Park. The site encompasses only a small portion of the Coleto Creek battlefield. The park includes an unmanned visitor's center, restroom facilities, and picnic area. Even now, the battlefield remains a dangerous place. Today's threat comes not from enemy soldiers, but rattlesnakes. Texas Parks and Wildlife maintains the site. (Photo by Deborah Bloys Hardin, Author's Collection)

incongruity had long since become the hallmark of the Texas government.

On 23 February, as Santa Anna's cannonballs began to hammer the walls of the Alamo, Bowie and Travis dispatched a letter that presented Fannin with a thorny dilemma. "In this extremity, we hope you will send us all the men you can spare promptly," the co-commanders explained. "We have but little provisions, but enough to serve us til you and your men arrive." Bowie and Travis concluded with words that seemed to question Fannin's honor – or, perhaps, his resolve: "We deem it unnecessary to repeat to a brave officer, who knows his duty, that we call on him for assistance." His volunteers urged Fannin to rush to the aid of their comrades in Béxar, but the Council had ordered him to hold Goliad. The situation required a swift decision, but faced with this necessity Fannin did what he did best. He vacillated.

This was the first true test of Fannin leadership, but he had already shown signs of cracking. He had jockeyed, plotted, and connived, for a field command. Now that he had it, he discovered to his horror that he was wholly out of his depth. As early as 14 February he had expressed self-doubt in a letter to Lieutenant Governor James Robinson and the Council. "I feel, I know, if you and the Council do not," he frankly admitted, "that I am incompetent." He continued, "I do most earnestly ask of you, and any real friend, to relieve me, and make a selection of one possessing all the requisites of a commander." On 21 February he again entreated Robinson. "I hope you will soon release me from the army, at least as an officer." Then, on the day before the siege of the Alamo began, he wrote Robinson with a final appeal. "I am a better judge of my military abilities than others," Fannin bemoaned, "and if I am qualified to command an Army, I have not found it out" – an attitude that must have inspired enormous confidence in his men.

On 26 February Fannin bowed to the demands of his volunteers and led 320 men and four cannon to relieve the Alamo garrison. Still in sight of Fort Defiance, a wheel came off a supply wagon. Just about the time

The Battle of Coleto Creek, 19 March 1836. Map showing positions of General Urrea, Colonel Fannin, Atascosita Road, US Cannon and Spanish Cannon, with Texian barricades. Goliad 10 miles; Coleto Creek 2 miles, Victoria 15 miles. Scale: 0–100 yds / 0–100 m.

the men repaired the first wagon, two more came apart. It became obvious that the oxen were too weak to haul the heavy artillery. Then a blue-tailed norther blew through. The sun was setting and Fannin rightly concluded that men could not march in the dark. He ordered them to stand down and return to their barracks. The soldiers returned to the fort in disgust. Fannin tried to keep spirits up. They would make a fresh start tomorrow, he cheerfully declared.

Yet the dawn revealed only more problems. The oxen had wandered off in the night. Fannin sent a few cowboys to round them up, but it was midday before they returned with the wayward beasts. Crestfallen, Fannin called a council of war. One disgruntled officer wondered if going to Béxar was such a good plan after all. The rest hastily agreed that it was not, for they had lost the stomach for any further relief expeditions. Fannin, who had always questioned the wisdom of a relief column, was palpably relieved. Béxar was 95 miles from Goliad; Fannin had managed to cover 250 yards.

Several writers have excoriated Fannin for failing to relieve the Alamo. From a strictly strategic standpoint, however, it is clear that marching to the relief of the Alamo would have been a mistake. On 28 February he learned of Johnson's rout at San Patricio. It was now apparent that another enemy force was driving up the Atascosito Road toward Goliad. That night he penned another letter to Robinson explaining his decision to abandon the Alamo relief effort: *It is obvious that the Enemy have entered Texas at two points, for the purpose of attacking Bexar and this place – The first has been attacked and we may expect the enemy here momentarily – Both places are important – and* this *at this time particularly so.*

The Alamo and Fort Defiance sat astride two vital approaches. Santa Anna did not even have to take the Alamo. Once he bottled up the defenders inside the fort, they were powerless to hinder his movements. He could dispatch his cavalrymen to sweep in behind Fannin and sever his communications to the settlements. And now, Fannin faced the additional threat from Urrea. He was in danger of being outflanked. Still, he had his orders from the Council. And while the Council had disbanded, it was the closest that Texas had to a government. It made little sense to rush to defend the Alamo while leaving the most direct approach into the Texian settlements open to Urrea. So Fannin remained at Goliad, waiting for someone in charge to tell him what to do, waiting for fate to overtake him.

On 13 or 14 March Fannin received orders that relieved him of the heavy burden of making a command decision. General Houston's orders were unequivocal. He instructed Fannin to abandon Fort Defiance and fall back to Victoria on the Guadalupe River. The general insisted that this be done "as soon as practicable." Apparently doubting Fannin's appreciation of the need for swift action, Houston repeated his directive in the strongest possible terms: "The immediate advance of the enemy may be confidently expected, as well as a rise of water. Prompt movements are therefore highly important." Notwithstanding Houston's orders, Fannin felt compelled to remain at Goliad until King and Ward returned from Refugio. They, of course, did not return, but as disaster loomed, Fannin sat and waited.

ABOVE **By the 1890s, Texans had mislaid the Coleto Creek battlefield. Based on his recollections of the spot that veterans had shown him years before, local rancher Sol Parks ostensibly located the center of Fannin's square. In 1894, Mr. Parks marked the spot with an old gin screw. In all its rusted glory, it remains there to this day as an unlikely battle memorial. (Photo by Deborah Bloys Hardin, Author's Collection)**

OPPOSITE **Texian soldiers greatly feared Mexican lances – and with good reason. The menacing configuration of this specimen suggests why. Captured at the Battle of Salado Creek in 1842, this weapon is on display at the Alamo. (Courtesy of the Daughters of the Republic of Texas Library at the Alamo, San Antonio, Texas)**

LEFT **At the battle of Coleto Creek, Fannin had ten pieces of artillery at his disposal. He placed his ordnance in the corners of a defensive square. This is one of Fannin's guns. This tube, and another like it, adorns the entrance to the Fannin Memorial in Goliad. (Photo by Deborah Bloys Hardin, Author's Collection)**

Fannin had long doubted his ability to command and soon his men began to share that opinion. "[T]he majority of the soldiers don't like him," Alabama volunteer Joseph G. Ferguson observed. "I don't know whether it is because they think he has not the interest of the country at heart or that he wishes to become great without taking the proper steps to attain greatness." Dr. Jack Shackelford, commander of the Alabama Red Rovers, criticized Fannin's earlier decision to reinforce Refugio. "Had he not done this," he later decried, "we should have been prepared to fall back on Victoria, as ordered, with a force sufficient to contend with every Mexican we might have encountered. Fannin's great anxiety, alone, for the fate of Ward and King, and their little band, delayed our march."

Several factors necessitated a swift withdrawal to Victoria. The Guadalupe River was a larger stream and thus more defensible than the San Antonio River. The Tejanos of Victoria were staunch federalists. The town provided much needed supplies and reinforcements were already there or on the march.

On 17 March Fannin learned of the fate of King and Ward. Instead of retreating immediately, he spent all of 18 March preparing to retreat. He insisted on hauling nine cannon and about 500 spare muskets. Lacking a sufficient number of draft horses, the garrison relied on oxen to haul baggage and artillery.

On 19 March Fannin finally began the march toward Victoria. But, even then, at a snail's pace. The oxen were "wild and contrary." Before they had traveled four miles, they stubbornly stopped to graze. Texian teamsters could only cuss and wait. Then a howitzer broke down, costing even more valuable time. The column had traveled only six miles when Fannin ordered a halt. Captain Shackelford "remonstrated warmly," but Fannin laughed off his concerns. He reassured Shackelford that Mexicans would never dare attack a force of more than 400 Texians.

Urrea was about to justify Shackleford's concerns. Tejano scouts had informed him that Fannin was abandoning Fort Defiance. The Mexican general had feared a lingering siege that would have absorbed time, men, and supplies. Now, however, he could catch the rebels on open ground and crush them in a single decisive action. He issued strict orders that his *soldados* in no way hinder Fannin while he made his error. But Urrea had another reason to delay. Following the fall of the Alamo, Santa Anna had dispatched elements of the Morales and San Luis battalions to Urrea. On 18 March those troops joined Urrea on the outskirts of Goliad. Those reinforcement increased Urrea's force to at least 1,400 *soldados*. And that total did not include the some 200 Tejano *rancheros* who flocked to the centralist banner. Urrea enjoyed both a tactical and numerical advantage. The time had come to spring his trap.

Meanwhile, Fannin had resumed his march after an hour's rest. The Texians had proceeded only a few miles when they observed a large force of enemy cavalry emerging from the timber two miles behind. Even then, Fannin insisted that the Mexican horsemen could do nothing but harass the retreat. Since his own cavalry galloped off toward Victoria, Fannin placed two gun crews to the rear with orders to delay the Mexican cavalry until his infantry could reach Coleto Creek some two miles ahead. Captains James Holland and Stephen Hurst unlimbered and loaded their guns as the bulk of Fannin's column

American illustrator Norman Price's pen-and-ink sketch captures accurately the disbelief of the Texian prisoners as their Mexican guards fire a volley into them. The captives believed that they were being marched to the coast where they would board ships bound for the United States. Some 342 fell victim to Santa Anna's barbarous order. (Courtesy of Texas State Library and Archives Commission)

Texans gather to commemorate those killed at the Battle of Coleto Creek and the Goliad Massacre. The monument marks the spot where soldiers under Thomas Jefferson Rusk buried the remains of Fannin and his men. The Mexican soldiers stripped the bodies and placed them on a pyre. The wood, however, was green and the fire went out, leaving the half-roasted corpses to the carrion. (Photo by Newton M. Warzecha. Courtesy Presidio La Bahía)

plodded forward. Fearing that the excitable oxen might bolt and take his wagons with them, Fannin actually instructed his men to advance slowly. He directed his attention on the enemy cavalrymen advancing on his rear, but now others appeared to the north and west. Urrea methodically directed his dragoons in for the kill.

Fannin recalled his guns and advanced toward a stand of timber about a mile to the northeast. Urrea's cavalry beat him to it. Seeing that the enemy had taken possession of the cover he sought, Fannin cast about for any advantage the terrain might offer – and found it. Some 500 yards to his front he detected a suggestion of a rise which might provide at least some benefit on this utterly flat ground. He shouted for his men to rush for the slight elevation. As they did so, however, an ammunition wagon broke down. Fannin would not abandon his ammo and directed his men to rally around their disabled wagon. This was the nightmare scenario for Texians: caught in the open without natural cover and surrounded by the Mexican cavalry.

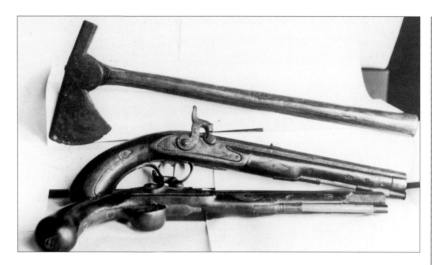

These weapons belonged to *Empresario* Stephen F. Austin, but were typical of those carried by Texian soldiers during the 1836 campaign. Observe that Austin has converted the flintlock pistols to accommodate a percussion lock. Officials of the *ad interim* Texas government ordered tomahawks such as the one here. The vengeful Texians employed them with vicious effect at San Jacinto. (Courtesy of the Prints and Photograph Collection, The Center for American History, University of Texas at Austin)

In a letter to Texas Secretary of War Thomas Jefferson Rusk, Houston wrote that news of Fannin's defeat produced the "darkest hours" of his life. Rusk latter carried authorization from President Burnet to relieve Houston, but supported the struggling general against his mutinous troops. He fought at San Jacinto and later served as a senator from Texas. (Author's Collection)

Fannin had his infantry form square. Positioning his cannon on each corner, he then moved his precious supply wagons inside the defensive barrier. As the Mexican cavalry swirled around the Texians, Urrea moved up his infantry. He gave his *cazadores* special targets – the draft animals. Urrea had Fannin and his rebels exactly where he wanted them and without oxen to pull their wagons, there they would remain. Once they had killed all the animals, the Mexican snipers turned their sights on the rebel artillerymen, then the rebel officers. Fannin went down as a ball tore through his thigh, but he was soon on his feet, shouting orders. James W. Fannin, Jr. was no Napoleon, but neither was he a coward.

The Texian rebels fought with a valor born of desperation. They displayed an abundance of guts, but lacked almost everything else. Gunners ran short of water to swab their guns. Expecting to arrive in Victoria by nightfall, they had packed little food. Their tactical position was the worst imaginable. The "cowardly" Mexicans had fought them to a standstill, killing nine Texians and wounding another 51.

That night Fannin and his officers took stock of their situation. They were surrounded; the noise of bugles and the derisive catcalls of enemy *soldados* confirmed that. In the darkness they might be able to cut their way through to the timber along the banks of Coleto Creek, but that meant abandoning the wounded. The enlisted men refused that option. As if to douse any flicker of hope, pouring rains ruined remaining supplies of gunpowder. Fannin had his men dig shallow trenches around the square and erect bulwarks of dead animals. Scraping sod at least kept the men warm as they toiled through the night.

Dawn revealed even more clearly the bleakness of the Texian position. During the night the rest of Urrea's troops arrived. He recorded that "one hundred infantry, two four-pounders, and a howitzer were added to my force." Armed with his howitzer Urrea could stand well beyond rifle range and pound the Texian square to red ruin. If the Texians broke and ran, the Mexican lancers stood ready to spit them like Christmas pigs.

Fannin hobbled forward under a white flag to discuss terms. Urrea made it clear that any surrender would be unconditional. Fannin conferred with his officers and assured them that he had received the best possible terms. Under such doleful circumstances, he was doubtless correct.

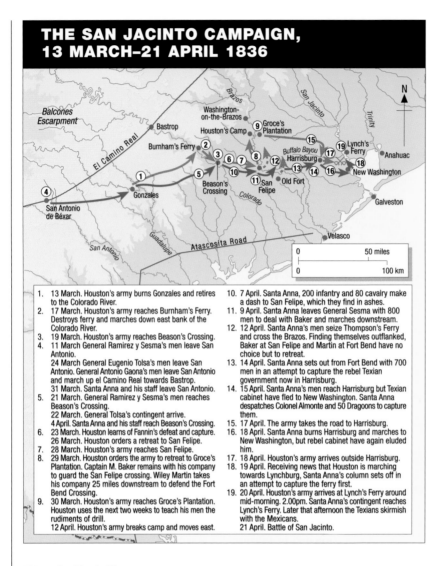

THE SAN JACINTO CAMPAIGN, 13 MARCH–21 APRIL 1836

1. 13 March. Houston's army burns Gonzales and retires to the Colorado River.
2. 17 March. Houston's army reaches Burnham's Ferry. Destroys ferry and marches down east bank of the Colorado River.
3. 19 March. Houston's army reaches Beason's Crossing.
4. 11 March General Ramirez y Sesma's men leave San Antonio.
   24 March General Eugenio Tolsa's men leave San Antonio. General Antonio Gaona's men leave San Antonio and march up el Camino Real towards Bastrop.
   31 March. Santa Anna and his staff leave San Antonio.
5. 21 March. General Ramirez y Sesma's men reaches Beason's Crossing.
   22 March. General Tolsa's contingent arrive.
   4 April. Santa Anna and his staff reach Beason's Crossing.
6. 23 March. Houston learns of Fannin's defeat and capture.
   26 March. Houston orders a retreat to San Felipe.
7. 28 March. Houston's army reaches San Felipe.
8. 29 March. Houston orders the army to retreat to Groce's Plantation. Captain M. Baker remains with his company to guard the San Felipe crossing. Wiley Martin takes his company 25 miles downstream to defend the Fort Bend Crossing.
9. 30 March. Houston's army reaches Groce's Plantation. Houston uses the next two weeks to teach his men the rudiments of drill.
   12 April. Houston's army breaks camp and moves east.
10. 7 April. Santa Anna, 200 infantry and 80 cavalry make a dash to San Felipe, which they find in ashes.
11. 9 April. Santa Anna leaves General Sesma with 800 men to deal with Baker and marches downstream.
12. 12 April. Santa Anna's men seize Thompson's Ferry and cross the Brazos. Finding themselves outflanked, Baker at San Felipe and Martin at Fort Bend have no choice but to retreat.
13. 14 April. Santa Anna sets out from Fort Bend with 700 men in an attempt to capture the rebel Texian government now in Harrisburg.
14. 15 April. Santa Anna's men reach Harrisburg but Texian cabinet have fled to New Washington. Santa Anna despatches Colonel Almonte and 50 Dragoons to capture them.
15. 17 April. The army takes the road to Harrisburg.
16. 18 April. Santa Anna burns Harrisburg and marches to New Washington, but rebel cabinet have again eluded him.
17. 18 April. Houston's army arrives outside Harrisburg.
18. 19 April. Receiving news that Houston is marching towards Lynchburg, Santa Anna's column sets off in an attempt to capture the ferry first.
19. 20 April. Houston's army arrives at Lynch's Ferry around mid-morning. 2.00pm. Santa Anna's contingent reaches Lynch's Ferry. Later that afternoon the Texians skirmish with the Mexicans.
   21 April. Battle of San Jacinto.

The Goliad Massacre

Urrea's victorious troops led the defeated Texians back to the fort that they had vacated only a day before. There they were held captive for a week. Then on 27 March *soldados* of the Yucatán and Tres Villas battalions led the prisoners out and gunned them down. Fannin and the other wounded could not march with the rest. Consequently, the Mexicans shot them inside the Presidio La Bahía. Urrea pleaded for the lives of Fannin and the other captives. "A gesture of generosity after such a hard-fought battle is most worthy of the most singular commendation," he implored Santa Anna, "and I can do no less than to commend it to your Excellency." But His Excellency would hear none of it. He dispatched a peremptory order to Lieutenant Colonel Nicolás de la Portilla, the officer that Urrea had left behind as post commander. A number of the surviving Texians noted Portilla's sorrow at having to carry out such a barbarous order. Indeed, he placed his own security at risk when he and other Mexican officers concocted reasons to strike 83 off the death list. Some 342 Texians perished in a fusillade of musketry, but 28 escaped. The *soldados*, most of whom were devout

US Army "Deserter". While formally neutral during the Texas Revolution, many soldiers of the US Army slipped across the Sabine River to assist the Texians. They appear to have done so with the tacit approval of their officers. The fellow illustrated here still sports his old sky-blue kersey uniform, but has been careful to strip it of all insignia that might identify him as a US regular. (Gary Zaboly, illustrator, from *Texian Iliad*. Author's Collection)

Roman Catholics, were horror struck that Santa Anna demanded that they perform this ghastly deed on a holy day. They would have been aware that 27 March was Palm Sunday.

Texians would ever remember the episode as the "Goliad Massacre". They believed that Fannin had secured assurances that the Mexican would treat his men as prisoners of war, which was patently untrue. Even so, Santa Anna could have acted with discretion, but chose otherwise. He would have done better to dump an army of defeated and demoralized volunteers on US shores. Their stories of Mexican compassion and Texian neglect would have dissuaded others from flocking to Texas. He might have gained the moral high ground, instead the world came to view him as a bloodthirsty butcher. Fannin and his men, moreover, joined the ranks of the Alamo defenders as martyrs whose blood called out for vengeance. Sam Houston's ragged soldiers, all that remained of the Texian Army, were preparing to answer that call.

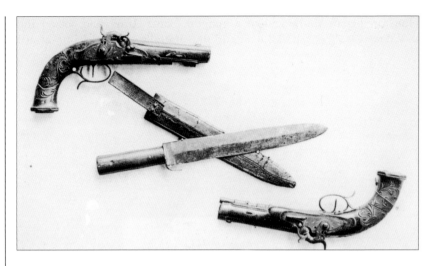

Weapons of San Jacinto veteran Peter Hansborough Bell. He fought as a private in Henry W. Karnes's cavalry company. Bell appears to have added percussion locks to what had formerly been flintlock pistols. Note the ornate carving on the pistol stocks, which contrasts sharply with the knife's makeshift appearance. Like many Texians, Bell parlayed his combat experience into a political career. In 1849, he won election as state governor. (Courtesy of the Texas State Library and Archives Commission)

HOUSTON'S RETREAT

While Santa Anna besieged the Alamo and Urrea advanced toward Goliad, Texian delegates gathered at Washington-on-the-Brazos. On 2 March – the very day that Urrea ambushed Dr. Grant – Texians declared their independence from Mexico. No longer would this be a civil war to restore the Constitution of 1824, but a struggle to ensure the security of the fledgling Republic of Texas. Among the delegates was Sam Houston. On 4 March the delegates reappointed Houston the military commander in chief. Houston insisted that the *ad interim* government award him authority over the regular army and the volunteers. For the first time, a single commander held legal authority over all men bearing arms in the cause of Texas.

Officials of the new Texas government urged Houston to rush to the rescue of the Alamo garrison. According to delegate Robert Coleman, however, General Houston "asserted publicly in the streets and grog shops of Washington that the letters received from our officers on the frontier were false and written by those officers for party purposes: that he well knew that there was not a Mexican near our border." Their general's incredulity notwithstanding, Texas officials finally ordered Houston to relieve Travis. Still, the general seemed in no hurry. During his ride from Washington to Gonzales, Houston halted at Burnam's Ferry on the Colorado River. According to settler W.W. Thompson, Houston lingered at Burnam's "all night & all day and all night again." While the fate of the Alamo wracked all Texians with apprehension, Houston was indifferent. When Thompson inquired about the plight of the Alamo defenders, he received an astounding reply. Houston "swore that he believed it to be a damn lie, & that all those reports from Travis and Fannin were lies, for there were no Mexican forces there and that he believed that it was only electioneering schemes on [the part of] Travis & Fannin to sustain their own popularity."

It seems incredible that Houston could actually have believed this. He was, however, a career politician – not a soldier. He weighed political considerations first and could not accept the possibility that there were those in Texas not involved in Byzantine power plays. By the time

David G. Burnet, *ad interim* president of the Republic of Texas, was a bitter detractor of Houston's withdrawal policy. "The enemy are laughing you to scorn," he admonished his general. "You must retreat no further. The country expects you to fight. The salvation of the country depends on your doing so." After the war, his dislike of Houston only increased. (Courtesy of the Prints and Photograph Collection, The Center for American History, University of Texas at Austin)

Erastus "Deaf" Smith was the Texians' ablest scout. He escorted Mrs. Dickinson and her infant daughter into Gonzales following the fall of the Alamo. On 18 April he captured a Mexican courier along with dispatches that revealed that Santa Anna had separated himself from his main force. That pilfered intelligence served as the foundation for all subsequent Texian strategy. (Courtesy of the Prints and Photograph Collection, The Center for American History, University of Texas at Austin)

Houston began thinking like a general, Santa Anna had seized the initiative, the Alamo had fallen, and the centralists were driving toward the Texian settlements.

On 11 March Houston finally arrived on the Guadalupe River at Gonzales to take command of the 374 volunteers gathered there to relieve the Alamo. Houston had no way of knowing that the Alamo garrison had been dead since 6 March. Indeed, he did not have that information confirmed until 13 March. On that date Alamo widow Suzanna Dickenson rode into town with details of the siege and the final assault. She further reported that Santa Anna and a 5,000-man force was en route toward Gonzales. Now that the Alamo had fallen, Santa Anna might easily sweep in behind Fannin down river at Goliad. With that in mind, Houston dispatched orders for Fannin to abandon his post and fall back to Victoria on the Guadalupe River.

All Houston's plans hinged upon Fannin's prompt withdrawal. With only 374 volunteers, Houston dared not engage Santa Anna at Gonzales. The rebel general sought to rendezvous with the Goliad garrison, for he was confident that with Fannin's 400 that he could halt the enemy's advance on the Colorado River.

On the night of 13 March, Houston began his retreat. His small contingent crossed the Colorado River on 17 March and took up position at Burnam's Ferry. Nevertheless, Houston soon realized that Burnam's was not the place to make his stand. Even if he did manage to halt Santa Anna's main force there, Urrea could ford the Colorado farther down river. Houston burned the ferry and marched down the east bank until reaching Beason's Crossing on 19 March.

Conditions improved at Beason's. Finally appreciating the seriousness of the threat, Texians flocked to Houston's banner, increasing his ranks to about 1,400 effectives. Spring rains swelled the Colorado River, temporally rendering it an impassable barrier for the *centralistas*. Santa Anna divided his forces, the better to locate the illusive rebels. If the Texians could not hope to fight the entire Mexican army, they might at least defeat an isolated detachment. Enraged at the reports of the Alamo slaughter, Texian volunteers were spoiling for a fight.

On 21 March they got their chance when an enemy division numbering between 600 and 800 under General Joaquín Ramírez y Sesma arrived opposite Beason's Crossing. The two forces glared at each other across the muddy waters of the Colorado River. His lieutenants urged Houston to cross the river and attack Ramírez before he could receive reinforcements. How often, they inquired, could they expect to fight at numerical advantage? Much to their dismay, however, Houston authorized only a reconnaissance. Houston wisely wished to wait for the arrival of Fannin's division, which he expected to join him at any time.

On 23 March, Houston learned of Fannin's surrender – news that totally upset his strategic planning. Writing Texas Secretary of War Thomas J. Rusk, Houston revealed the depth of his despair: *You know I am not easily depressed, but before my God, since we parted, I have found the darkest hours of my past life! If what I have learned from Fannin be true, I deplore it and can only attribute the ill luck to his attempt to retreat in daylight in the face of a superior force. He is an ill-fated man.*

On 26 March Houston ordered a retreat to San Felipe on the Brazos River – a command his soldiers greeted with derision. With his

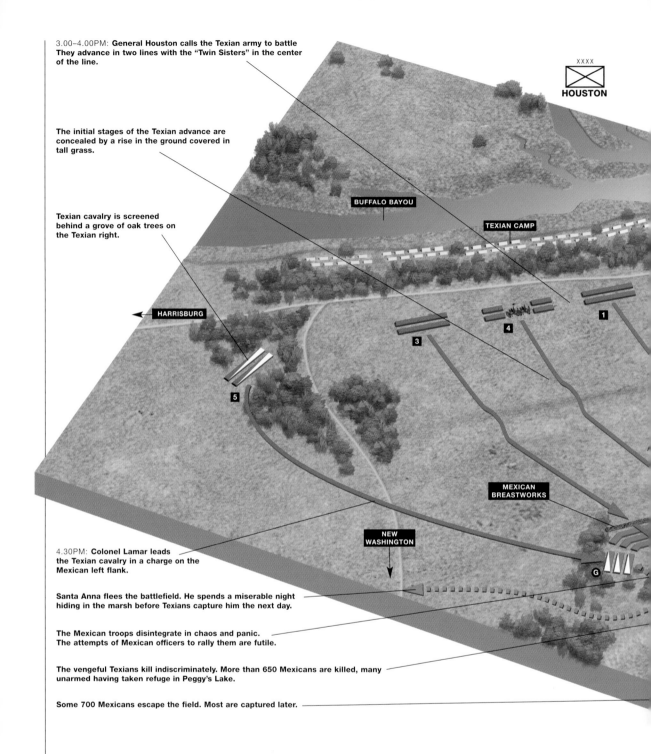

3.00–4.00PM: **General Houston calls the Texian army to battle** They advance in two lines with the "Twin Sisters" in the center of the line.

The initial stages of the Texian advance are concealed by a rise in the ground covered in tall grass.

Texian cavalry is screened behind a grove of oak trees on the Texian right.

HOUSTON

BUFFALO BAYOU

TEXIAN CAMP

◄— **HARRISBURG**

1

4

3

5

MEXICAN BREASTWORKS

NEW WASHINGTON

4.30PM: **Colonel Lamar leads** the Texian cavalry in a charge on the Mexican left flank.

G

Santa Anna flees the battlefield. He spends a miserable night hiding in the marsh before Texians capture him the next day.

The Mexican troops disintegrate in chaos and panic. The attempts of Mexican officers to rally them are futile.

The vengeful Texians kill indiscriminately. More than 650 Mexicans are killed, many unarmed having taken refuge in Peggy's Lake.

Some 700 Mexicans escape the field. Most are captured later.

THE BATTLE OF SAN JACINTO, 21 APRIL 1836

Viewed from the southwest showing the Texians storming the Mexican camp and the rout of the Mexican troops into Peggy's Lake.

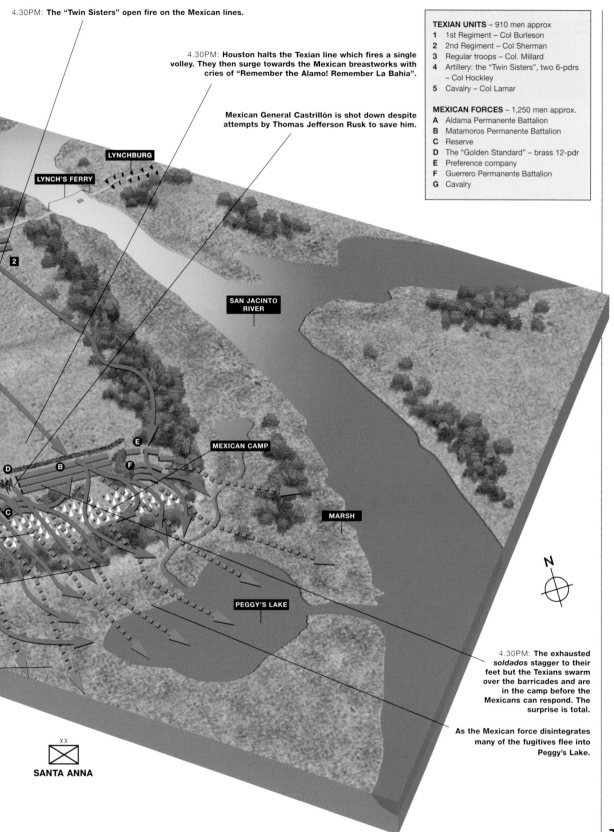

4.30PM: **The "Twin Sisters" open fire on the Mexican lines.**

4.30PM: **Houston halts the Texian line which fires a single volley. They then surge towards the Mexican breastworks with cries of "Remember the Alamo! Remember La Bahía".**

Mexican General Castrillón is shot down despite attempts by Thomas Jefferson Rusk to save him.

TEXIAN UNITS – 910 men approx
1 1st Regiment – Col Burleson
2 2nd Regiment – Col Sherman
3 Regular troops – Col. Millard
4 Artillery: the "Twin Sisters", two 6-pdrs
  – Col Hockley
5 Cavalry – Col Lamar

MEXICAN FORCES – 1,250 men approx.
A Aldama Permanente Battalion
B Matamoros Permanente Battalion
C Reserve
D The "Golden Standard" – brass 12-pdr
E Preference company
F Guerrero Permanente Battalion
G Cavalry

LYNCHBURG

LYNCH'S FERRY

2

SAN JACINTO RIVER

E

D   B   F

MEXICAN CAMP

C

MARSH

PEGGY'S LAKE

N

4.30PM: **The exhausted** *soldados* **stagger to their feet but the Texians swarm over the barricades and are in the camp before the Mexicans can respond. The surprise is total.**

As the Mexican force disintegrates many of the fugitives flee into Peggy's Lake.

X X
SANTA ANNA

Sidney Sherman instigated the skirmish on 20 April and commanded the Second Regiment of the Texian army the following day at the Battle of San Jacinto. During the 1836 campaign he became a bitter critic of Houston's generalship and remained so for the rest of his life. (Author's Collection)

leadership in question, Houston weighed his strategic options. If he attacked Ramírez, across a swollen river and against entrenchments, Houston risked inflicting such damage on his own force that it would be incapable of facing future opponents. Moreover, what if Santa Anna or Urrea moved in on his flanks? The Texians would then have to fight a superior force with their backs to a river. The only reasonable course was to retreat to the Brazos, keep the rebel army intact, and pray that Santa Anna made a mistake.

The Texian army reached San Felipe on 28 March but, after spending only one night there, Houston ordered yet another retreat to Jared Groce's plantation about 20 miles upriver. The abandonment of San Felipe created a storm of protest. Two companies bluntly refused to withdraw any further. Captain Mosely Baker's command remained to guard the San Felipe crossing of the Brazos River; Wiley Martin took his company 25 miles down river to defend the Fort Bend ford. Disgusted with Houston and his policy of retreat, many of his volunteers deserted the army to assist their families. Most Texian women and children had fled in what they called the "Runaway Scrape", a wild exodus toward the Louisiana border. On 29 March, the day Houston began the retreat to Groce's plantation, the Texian army had dwindled to a mere 500 troops.

But Houston used the following two weeks at Groce's to good advantage. There he drilled his men in the rudiments of linear formations. Austrian-born George Erath admitted that the "delay at Groce's had a good effect in disciplining us and in giving us information on military tactics." Through the heroic efforts of the Texian surgeons, most of those stricken with maladies brought on by their almost constant exposure to spring rains gradually improved.

The Texian rebels may have regained their health and confidence, but not their faith in Houston. Many spoke openly of overthrowing Houston if he did not soon order an offensive movement. Texas politicians were equally dismayed with their retreating general. *Ad interim* President David G. Burnet addressed a scathing letter to Houston. *Sir: The enemy are laughing you to scorn. You must fight them. You must retreat no further. The country expects you to fight. The salvation of the country depends on your doing so.*

On 12 April, Houston broke camp at Groce's. It required two days to transport all the men, animals, and supplies to the east bank of the Brazos River. The general then marched the army eastward, but gave no hint of its destination. Nearly all the rebel soldiers hoped that they were heading toward the enemy. At the same time, they were fearful that Houston was leading them to the Sabine River and shameful safety. Houston maintained his silence and rode eastward.

On 16 April the Texian army reached a major crossroads. The north road led to Nacogdoches and safety, the other toward Harrisburg and confrontation. Tension rose as the army approached the forks of the road. Many swore they would refuse if the general ordered them north. As the moment of decision approached, the general lingered toward the rear. As the lead elements drew near the forks, a cry resounded through ranks: "To the right, boys, to the right." The willful revolutionaries took the road to Harrisburg; Houston tagged along.

The question has been asked ever since whether Houston intended to march to Harrisburg. He and his partisans always claimed that he did, but Dr. Anson Jones, a Texian surgeon, believed otherwise. "Gen. Houston's policy was to retreat beyond the Neches [River] and beyond a line which Gen. Gains, of the United States Army, would have defended," he recalled, "but [Houston] was forced by the men of his army to depart from this policy, and go to Lynchburg, from which resulted the battle of San Jacinto."

An incident along the Harrisburg Road corroborated the assertions that Houston intended to march away from the enemy. At Groce's plantation, Pamela Mann had loaned the army a team of prized oxen. Mrs. Mann expressed concern for her animals, but the general assured her that he was taking the army – and her oxen – to Nacogdoches and out of harm's way. Upon learning that the rebels had turned toward Harrisburg, she rode after her property. Riding up to Houston, she shouted, "General, you told me a damn lie. You said you was going on the Nacogdoches Road." As Private Robert Hancock Hunter told it, Mrs. Mann charged Houston with duplicity: "I loaned you the oxen to go to the Trinity; as you have changed your route, I shall take them." With that, the widow cut her oxen from the traces and led them away. Perhaps Mrs. Mann should not have been so hard on Houston. After all, when he had told her at Groce's that he intended to march in the opposite direction, he had meant it. His soldiers, however, had other ideas.

The most compelling confirmation comes from Houston himself. In 1845 he addressed a loving crowd in his namesake city. On that day, at least, he was remarkably candid:

In the course of two days [at Gonzales] I received the lamentable information that Colonel Travis and his noble compatriots had succumbed to overwhelming numbers and had been brutally slaughtered … I then determined to retreat and get as near to Andrew Jackson and the old flag as I could. [Author's emphasis]

What a remarkable admission this is. If Houston was telling the truth, he never intended to fight on the Colorado, nor the Brazos, nor did he plan to veer south at the forks of the road. So, when he repeatedly swore that he planned to defend the Texas settlements, did Houston lie to his men and his government? The evidence suggests that he did.

Yet, what of Santa Anna's movements? Following his victory at the Alamo, he had no information of Houston's whereabouts. He had to find the rebel army before he could crush it. To that end he divided his army into smaller hunting parties. Urrea was to continue his sweep of the coastal prairies, while he dispatched General Antonio Gaona up Camino Real toward Bastrop. He would follow General Ramírez y Sesma to Beason's Crossing on the Colorado River. He followed Houston to San Felipe on the Brazos River, but when Houston marched up river toward Groce's, Santa Anna tired of this game of hide-and-seek. He no longer considered Houston's contingent a serious threat. Dispatching orders to Filisola, Urrea, and Gaona to concentrate near Old Fort on the lower Brazos River, Santa Anna moved down river from San Felipe. If all the units arrived at Old Fort, he would have some 3,400 men – more than three times the size of Houston's force.

When he arrived near Old Fort, Santa Anna learned that the *ad interim* Texian government was in Harrisburg, only 30 miles away. But to capture the rebel leaders, he would have to travel light and fast. Compulsively, he placed himself at the head of only 500 men and

During the skirmishing on 20 April, Jesse Billingsley led his company out in support of Sherman in deliberate defiance of Houston's orders. Following the war he became a vociferous critic of Houston's conduct during the 1836 campaign. Billingsley accused the general of "willfully lying" and asserted that he had "assumed to himself credit that was due to others." (Courtesy of the Prints and Photographs Collection, The Center for American History, University of Texas at Austin)

OVERLEAF
HENRY ARTHUR MCARDLE'S *BATTLE OF SAN JACINTO*. Painted during the 1870s, the canvas accurately depicts the weather, topography, and equipment on the day of battle. The artist interviewed many veterans of the battle – including Santa Anna. His notebooks, preserved by the Texas State Library in Austin, constitute an invaluable source for the student of the battle. (Courtesy of the Texas State Library and Archives Commission)

dashed toward Harrisburg. When Santa Anna arrived there on 15 April, he found that the Texian officials had already abandoned the town and were bound for Galveston Bay. He hastened his cavalry in pursuit, but they were too late. President Burnet and his cabinet had made their getaway to Galveston Island. The escape of the rebel government disappointed Santa Anna, but he could take solace that he had forced the "perfidious foreigners" off Texas soil. All that remained was to rejoin his main force near Old Fort. To accomplish that, he would need to take the Harrisburg Road near the site of Lynch's Ferry at the point where Buffalo Bayou flowed into the San Jacinto River.

Tejano Volunteer, Seguín's Company. Houston worried that, once the fighting at San Jacinto began, his vindictive soldiers might not discriminate between the enemy and their Tejano allies. This man, therefore, makes himself conspicuous by the white pasteboard in his hatband. Seguín's men acquitted themselves gallantly, transforming those odd bits of pasteboard into unit battle honors. (Gary Zaboly, illustrator, from *Texian Iliad*. Author's Collection)

LEFT In a panic to escape the murderous Texians, many Mexican soldiers at San Jacinto pitched headlong into a boggy pool called Peggy's Lake. Texians stood on the bank and shot their ill-fated foes like fish in a barrel. The muddy waters turned crimson. One Mexican survivor lamented: "It was here that the greatest carnage took place." (*Massacre at Peggy's Lake, San Jacinto Battlefield, April 21, 1836*, by Charles Shaw. From the collection of the Star of the Republic Museum)

On 18 April Houston's favorite scout, Erastus "Deaf" Smith, captured a Mexican courier and with him a windfall of dispatches. The letters revealed that Santa Anna was at the head of a diminutive force. More important, the Texians now knew Santa Anna's exact whereabouts. His Excellency still believed Houston to be camped at Groce's along the Brazos. If Houston struck before Santa Anna rejoined his main force, he would enjoy a numerical advantage. This was his only opportunity to win the war with a single knockout punch. If Houston could kill or capture Santa Anna, he might win all with one roll of the dice.

On the evening of 19 April the Texian army crossed to the west bank of Buffalo Bayou about $2\frac{1}{2}$ miles below Harrisburg. Houston left those who were too ill to be effective – some 248 men – opposite Harrisburg to guard the baggage. Houston knew that Santa Anna's detachment was traveling along the New Washington road toward Lynch's Ferry. It now became a race to reach the ferry. The following morning the Texians marched up the Harrisburg Road toward Lynch's Ferry. They arrived about mid-morning; the enemy was nowhere in sight. Houston had won the race. Texians pitched their camp in the woods along Buffalo Bayou and awaited the arrival of His Excellency.

THE BATTLE OF SAN JACINTO

That afternoon, upon his arrival at Lynch's Ferry, Santa Anna received the shock of his life. Instead of skulking at Groce's plantation, the rebel army stood between him and the bulk of his army. This was serious; how could he have so misjudged Houston? Santa Anna immediately dispatched a rider to Fort Bend. He sent orders to Cos to march to his aid with as many men as he could muster. Then he had his men make camp about $\frac{3}{4}$ mile from the Texian position. The *soldados* busied themselves erecting breastworks around their camp. Would Cos arrive in time?

Across the field, Texians were itching for battle. Skirmishing began with an exchange of artillery fire. Former Alamo commander, J.C. Neill brought up two matching 6-pdrs, which the Texians called the "Twin Sisters". Mexicans gunners replied with a brass 12-pdr, their only ordnance. Neill caught a canister round in the fleshy part of his hip, but the Mexicans withdrew their cannon into a dense wood.

Sidney Sherman sought Houston's permission to deploy his cavalry to reconnoiter the Mexican position. Houston assented, but ordered that Sherman was not to bring on a general action. Sherman agreed – and then led his troopers in a spirited charge on the Mexican camp. Santa Anna met the threat with his dragoons. The superior Mexican cavalry were mauling Sherman's horsemen. Back in the Texian camp, his men begged Houston to send in infantry support. Houston steadfastly refused to send infantry to assist the insubordinate Sherman.

LEFT While not as common as those cast in lead, excavations of Mexican campsites in the *Mar de Lodo* have uncovered several brass canister rounds. Primary accounts maintained that a copper ball shattered Houston's ankle. That is doubtful, since archeologists have not located any copper rounds. It is more likely that specimens such as these injured the general. It was a natural mistake; slathered in blood, brass would closely resemble copper. (Courtesy of the Houston Archeological Society)

A French-Canadian, Dr. Nicholas Descomps Labadie left one of the most colorful and detailed accounts of the San Jacinto Campaign. (Courtesy of the Prints and Photograph Collection, The Center for American History, University of Texas at Austin)

Standard of the Toluca Battalion. The Batallon Activa de Toluca was part of Colonel Francisco Duque's column at the Alamo, where it suffered terrible casualties. The battalion saw action again at San Jacinto. It was there that the Texians captured their standard. It has remained in Texas ever since. Today it is part of the Flag Collection at the Texas State Library. (Courtesy of the Texas State Library and Archives Commission)

Captain Jesse Billingsley did not stand on ceremony. Ignoring Houston's orders, he led his company onto the field. To reach their beleaguered comrades, the unit had to march directly in front of Houston. Red faced, the general instructed Billingsley to countermarch to the safety of the timber. "This order the men treated with derision," Billingsley laughingly recounted, "requesting him to countermarch himself, if he desired it, and steadily held on their way to the support of Col Sherman, and succeeded in driving the enemy behind their breastworks."

While exciting, the skirmishing of 20 April achieved nothing. As night fell, many Texians loudly wondered why Houston had not attacked. Here were the Mexicans; the Texians had the numbers. Why was Houston waiting?

At 9.00 the following morning they had even more reason to wonder why Houston did not act. General Cos reinforced Santa Anna with about 540 troops. The Mexican force swelled to some 1,200 *soldados*. Houston's 910 Texians no longer enjoyed numerical superiority. Houston ordered "Deaf" Smith to destroy Vince's Bridge on the Harrisburg Road. The destruction of the bridge would hamper the arrival of additional enemy reinforcements, but it also severed the Texians' main line of retreat.

Standard of the Batallon Matamoros Permanente. The permanent (regular) Matamoros Battalion was among the few Mexican units to have fought at the Alamo, Coleto Creek, and – to their great misfortune – San Jacinto. At this last engagement, Texian rebels decimated the unit and captured its standard. The banner has recently undergone extensive restoration. This image, of course, displays the pre-restoration standard. (Courtesy of the Texas State Library and Archives Commission)

About noon, Houston held a council of war. What really occurred remains a mystery. Houston partisans claim that he ordered the attack, shouting "the sun of Austerlitz has risen again!" His detractors avow that Rusk and the other officers insisted on an attack without delay. Finally they simply wore him down. According to Robert Coleman, Houston bitterly exclaimed, "Fight then and be damned!"

Whatever his true intentions, Houston called the army to battle between 3.00pm and 4.00pm. The rebels advanced in two lines, with the Twin Sisters in the middle and the cavalry screened behind an oak grove on the Mexican left. Advancing with the rebels were 19 Tejanos of Captain Juan Seguín's company. Most hailed from Béxar and all had lost friends at the Alamo. Now on the day of battle they, no less than their American neighbors, wanted a chance for revenge.

Across the field, Santa Anna decided that if the rebels had not attacked by now, they were not likely to do so. Besides, his *soldados* were dead on their feet. Cos's reinforcements had marched throughout the previous night, while his own men had been awake for almost 33 hours. His Excellency ordered his troops to stand down. The men collapsed in exhausted heaps.

The Texians attacked the camp about 4.30pm. Disoriented *soldados* stumbled to their feet, but already the rebels were among them. Surprise was complete. As one of their officers described it the Mexican soldiers became a "panic-stricken herd." Shouting their battle cry, "Remember the Alamo – Remember La Bahía," the Texians swept the Mexican camp. The actual battle lasted 18 minutes, but the slaughter lasted much longer.

Determined to avenge the defeats at the Alamo and Goliad, the Texians committed atrocities that were at least as reprehensible as those

Standard of the Batallon Guerrero. For the victorious Texians, the Battle of San Jacinto provided a windfall of captured standards. When one compares the three captured standards, it becomes readily apparent that enormous variety existed in the design of each unit's banner. Although not apparent here, this one has also received a much-needed restoration. (Courtesy of the Texas State Library and Archives Commission)

of the Mexicans. *Soldados* cast down their muskets and threw up their hands, all the while screaming "Me no Alamo – Me no Goliad." It availed them nothing; the Texians gunned them down. Dr. Nicholas Labadie was attempting to take a Mexican officer prisoner when an enraged Texian shoved him aside and shot the man in the face. Blood and brains splattered Labadie's clothing. Ashamed, the doctor later bemoaned that he had "witnessed acts of cruelty which I forbear to recount."

The bloodletting continued. Texas rebels killed until they were too exhausted to kill anymore. Some 650 Mexicans fell victim to their rage. About 700 escaped the field, only to be taken captive later. Texian casualties were nine killed and 30 wounded. Among the wounded was General Houston. A brass Mexican canister round had smashed his ankle to powder.

The Texians ransacked the Mexican camp, appropriating horses, muskets, shoes, sabers, and $12,000 in silver. The rebels also took a

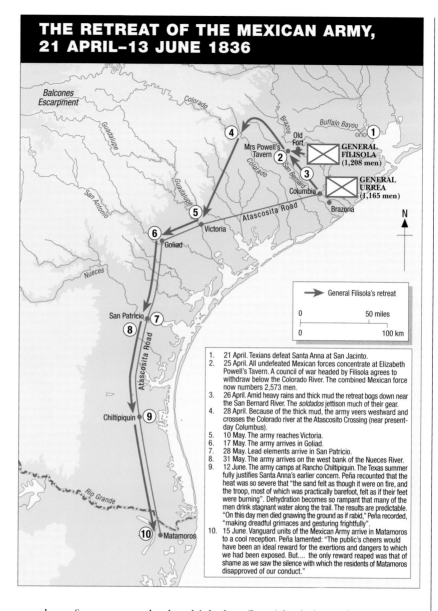

THE RETREAT OF THE MEXICAN ARMY, 21 APRIL–13 JUNE 1836

GENERAL FILISOLA (1,208 men)

GENERAL URREA (1,165 men)

General Filisola's retreat

| 0 | | 50 miles |
| 0 | | 100 km |

1. 21 April. Texians defeat Santa Anna at San Jacinto.
2. 25 April. All undefeated Mexican forces concentrate at Elizabeth Powell's Tavern. A council of war headed by Filisola agrees to withdraw below the Colorado River. The combined Mexican force now numbers 2,573 men.
3. 26 April. Amid heavy rains and thick mud the retreat bogs down near the San Bernard River. The *soldados* jettison much of their gear.
4. 28 April. Because of the thick mud, the army veers westward and crosses the Colorado river at the Atascosito Crossing (near present-day Columbus).
5. 10 May. The army reaches Victoria.
6. 17 May. The army arrives in Goliad.
7. 28 May. Lead elements arrive in San Patricio.
8. 31 May. The army arrives on the west bank of the Nueces River.
9. 12 June. The army camps at Rancho Chiltipiquin. The Texas summer fully justifies Santa Anna's earlier concern. Peña recounted that the heat was so severe that "the sand felt as though it were on fire, and the troop, most of which was practically barefoot, felt as if their feet were burning". Dehydration becomes so rampant that many of the men drink stagnant water along the trail. The results are predictable. "On this day men died gnawing the ground as if rabid," Peña recorded, "making dreadful grimaces and gesturing frightfully".
10. 15 June. Vanguard units of the Mexican Army arrive in Matamoros to a cool reception. Peña lamented: "The public's cheers would have been an ideal reward for the exertions and dangers to which we had been exposed. But.... the only reward reaped was that of shame as we saw the silence with which the residents of Matamoros disapproved of our conduct."

number of enemy standards, which they flourished about the camp. But the real prize came the following day. On 22 April James A. Sylvester found a Mexican soldier shivering in a swamp. When Sylvester brought his captive into camp, the restlessness of the other Mexican prisoners gave away his true identity. His Excellency had fled the field the day before and was attempting to pose as a common *soldado*. The Texian soldiers roughly hauled him before the wounded Houston. Through an interpreter, Santa Anna complimented his rival. "That man may consider himself born to no common destiny who has conquered the Napoleon of the West," he purred. "And now it remains for him to be generous to the vanquished."

"You should have remembered that at the Alamo," Houston snarled.

Houston, however, did not execute Santa Anna – although there were many who urged him to. Ever the politician, he realized that a captive tyrant could be a powerful diplomatic card. Furthermore,

William Henry Huddle's *The Surrender of Santa Anna* (1886). In this painting Surgeon General Dr. Alexander H. Ewing dresses the shattered ankle of General Sam Houston. Erastus "Deaf" Smith, chief scout of the Texian army, sits nearby and strains to hear his wounded general. Houston offers the captured Santa Anna a seat on an ammunition box. Clearly, vengeful Texians are eager to hang the Mexican dictator from the nearest limb. (Courtesy of Texas State Library and Archives Commission)

Houston feared that Filisola or Urrea, who still greatly outnumbered his force, might launch their own attacks. The Texians had accomplished a minor miracle; their general doubted they could do it twice. In return for his life, Santa Anna dispatched orders to Filisola to retire to Victoria. Remarkably, Filisola obeyed them.

Filisola's Withdrawal

On 23 April news of Santa Anna's defeat and capture reached Filisola at Old Fort. On 25 April Filisola called a council of war at the tavern belonging to Elizabeth Powell. Urrea and the other generals present agreed that the army should retire below the Colorado River and attempt to establish communications with the Mexican government. At that juncture, the movement was a strategic withdrawal. Filisola had every intention of continuing the campaign after the army had regrouped and refitted.

Yet, what awaited the Mexican *soldados* was worse than anything they had experienced. During the march, rains began to fall. By the time they reached the San Bernard River bottom the boggy ground made any kind of travel all but impossible. The Mexicans recalled the area as the "*Mar de Lodo*" – the Sea of Mud. Men sank to their knees; each step became an ordeal. They began to jettison everything that weighed them down: shells, round shot, canister, and even entire boxes of nails. Some even tossed their muskets. To make matters worse, many *soldados* came down with dysentery. The "Mar de Lodo" sapped what morale the army had left. Filisola always maintained that it was not the rebels who defeated the once proud Army of Operations, but the "inclemency of the season … made still more unattractive by the rigor of the climate and the character of the land." Consequently, Filisola retreated not to Victoria, but across the Rio Grande. Many in the army condemned his actions, but there was little doubt that he had made the prudent decision. The bedraggled *soldados* who crossed the Rio Grande could take some degree of solace that it had not been the Texians who had brought them low, but rather the land of Texas itself.

AFTERMATH

Texians claimed to have "won" their independence at San Jacinto. The rancorous history of the Republic of Texas reveals this as something of an exaggeration. The United States, Great Britain, and France all recognized Texas independence. Mexicans, however, still considered Texas a part of their republic. Even though the province was in open rebellion, even though *norteamericanos* inhabited the territory, Mexicans vowed that some day, when conditions permitted, they would recapture the land they knew as Tejas.

In 1842, two Mexican forays embarrassed and angered citizens of the Texas Republic. While these raids proved bothersome, they also revealed a comforting reality. The Mexican government was simply too weak to take and hold ground north of the Rio Grande; these brief border raids were the best they could manage. The Mexican army hoped, however, that they would be enough to keep their claims of possession alive and thwart American annexation plans. These hopes proved forlorn and in December 1845 the United States finalized the annexation of Texas – a process which led to the Mexican-American War.

Many Mexicans blamed Santa Anna, with some justification, for losing Texas. After a brilliant forced march that achieved strategic surprise, His Excellency became complacent. Following the fall of the Alamo, he lingered far too long in Béxar. Disdainful of the rebel army, he made a fatal blunder in separating his detachment for the fruitless drive on Harrisburg. When he did, the Texians were able to exploit his mistake. Nevertheless, the error was Santa Anna's. Houston was able to surprise the Mexicans on 21 April only because Santa Anna had exhausted his troops and neglected his camp security. His Excellency had, furthermore, moved his army off the prairies where his superior cavalry had the edge and ventured into wooded marshlands where the Texians could employ the terrain to their advantage. In the final analysis, San Jacinto was not so much a battle Sam Houston won, but rather one that Santa Anna botched.

Nor does Houston emerge as a brilliant strategist. The Alamo had fallen before he was willing to admit that the Mexicans were on Texas soil. By his own admission, he never intended to give battle at San Jacinto. The Texian rebels hauled their general kicking and screaming to the banks of Buffalo Bayou.

When all the tales are told, however, it is the men of the Alamo that we remember. And that is as it should be. One comes to appreciate that the soldiers – on both sides of the wall – were individuals far from home, confronted with a deeply unpleasant task, and feverishly wishing to be somewhere else. But even when one strips away the layers of myth and mawkish chauvinism, what is left remains grandly heroic. Those men do not require fabrication to keep them green in our collective memory. Ultimately, their heroism endures. No, it does more than endure – It shines.

The Alamo church as it currently appears. Nestled in the heart of a bristling modern city, the Alamo is the state's most frequently visited tourist attraction. Some 2.5 million visitors come from all over the world to stand before those old stones and honor the courage and sacrifice of the defenders. Even in our cynical age, the place and its history still possess the power to inspire. (Photo by Keith Durham. Author's Collection)

THE BATTLEFIELDS
TODAY

THE ALAMO

The sands of time have severely eroded the Alamo battlefield. In 1836 the main plaza of the fort contained almost three acres, making the defensive perimeter just under a quarter of a mile long. The extensive compound that thwarted Santa Anna for 13 days is long gone. Nowadays, the Alamo no longer resembles a fort; manicured lawns, fishponds, and towering shade trees provide the appearance of a park – a tranquil haven amidst a bustling city. Not that it's unpleasant, it's just not what one expects. Film historian Frank Thompson echoes the frustration of many modern tourists: "Visitors want a battleground; instead they find a shrine. The Alamo as it now stands is, in a very real sense, no longer itself, but a monument to itself."

Given all that, should one even bother to visit the Alamo? Yes, by all means! Notwithstanding urban sprawl and maudlin interpretations, those old stones retain their ability to awe and inspire. The challenge then is to reconstruct the 1836 battlefield in one's mind. It is possible, and this book – with a little imagination – will greatly assist the visitor.

Trip Preparation

Anyone anticipating a visit to the Alamo should consult two outstanding web sites. The first, www.thealamo.org, is the official site maintained by the Alamo custodians, the Daughters of the Republic of Texas (DRT). The second, *Alamo de Parras*, is far and away the best Alamo site on the web. It incorporates history, a teacher's guide, frequently asked questions, book reviews, interviews with authors, and an archive section which includes original articles by leading scholars. Its web address is http://alamo-de-parras.welkin.org

Those wishing to correspond with the Alamo staff may write to:

The Alamo
300 Alamo Plaza
San Antonio, Texas
78299

One may telephone at (210) 225-1391, or send a Fax transmission at (210) 229-1343.

In San Antonio

Those unfamiliar with San Antonio might find getting to the Alamo somewhat daunting. Not to worry; every cabdriver knows the way and the highway signs are difficult to miss. Parking is available at several pay lots in the vicinity. The Alamo is located at 300 Alamo Plaza in downtown

San Antonio. It is open to visitors every day except Christmas Eve and Christmas Day. Hours are 9.00am to 5.30pm Monday through Saturday. Sunday hours are 10.00am to 5.30pm.

The Alamo is the number one tourist attraction in Texas. During peak vacation periods, thousands of sightseers pass through its doors on any given day. To enjoy your visit fully, plan on arriving first thing in the morning before the crowd assembles. Also be sure to visit the Alamo at night. It is not open to visitors, of course, but the site assumes a distinct ambiance in moonlight.

For those who have the luxury of choosing their vacation time, the best time to visit is the week of 6 March. During the weekend closest to that date one can view and even participate in a number of commemorative events. These include living history programs and the annual meetings of the Alamo Battlefield Association and the Alamo Society. Aficionados refer to the period from 2 March (Texas Independence Day) to 6 March as the "High Holy Days". Anyone with the slightest interest in the battle should attend High Holy Days at least once in his lifetime. It is an experience.

On the Alamo Grounds

The best place to begin your tour is not actually at the Alamo. When showing friends about, I always start at the Rivercenter Mall located some 200 paces southeast of the church. It is the home of the San Antonio IMAX theatre that several times each day features *Alamo ... The Price of Freedom*. While the movie is a bit too fond of myth, it remains the most historically accurate representation on film. The venue is truly spectacular; the theater seats up to 425 patrons and boasts a 61 x 84ft screen and a 32-speaker component, six-track sound system. When the cannon blasts, you may wish to cover your ears! Be sure to inspect the displays of historic uniforms and weapons in the lobby. Readers of this volume will have a solid understanding of the historical context, but it is a fair bet that you may be traveling with children or a spouse who will require a quick introduction to the battle. This film does that nicely.

After viewing the film, it is a good idea to walk the original perimeter of the fort. The Bird's-eye Views on pages 38-39 and 46-47 will prove valuable at this juncture. Starting at the south corner of the church, walk across Plaza de Valero and across Alamo Street. City officials have reconstructed a portion of the southwest corner of the 1836 compound. Standing here one begins to appreciate the fort's enormous size. Looking north, the row of buildings approximates the location of the west wall. From the southwest corner bastion you can actually see the Plexiglas display that protects a portion of the original west wall foundations.

Next, walk northward along the sidewalk toward Houston Street. Across the street you will see the modern post office. The post office steps mark the location of the north wall battery where Travis fell. Cross Houston Street again into Plaza de Valero; inspect the Alamo cenotaph designed by Pompeo Coppini in 1939.

Stroll eastward along Houston Street past the Long Barracks. Enter the north gate of the Alamo complex. You will immediately see the Gift Shop/Museum, but delay entering; better to see it last. Instead turn right into the Cavalry Courtyard. The DRT has turned this area into an artillery park. Here the visitor can see many of the guns used during the

1836 siege, including the famous 18-pdr and the stubby gunade. On the Alamo grounds, be sure to look for the exceptional point-of-focus signage. Designed by illustrator Gary Zaboly (whose considerable talents readers of this book will already be familiar with), each sign reveals to viewers what the Alamo fort would have looked like if they were to have been standing on that exact spot in 1836. Zaboly and the DRT deserve commendation for their insight; more than any other interpretive tool, these signs allow visitors to reconstruct the historic fort in their mind's eye.

Walk through the gate into the Covento Courtyard. From there enter the Long Barracks Museum. Here in the dim quarters of the Long Barracks some of the bloodiest fighting took place. In rooms where soldiers grappled and died, visitors now view displays showcasing a variety of Alamo related artifacts. These include period weapons, uniforms, and personal items. Of the original 1836 complex only the heavily restored Long Barracks and the church remain. Visitors should be aware that one enters and exits the Long Barracks through rear doors. The DRT has blocked the 1836 doors that faced the main plaza and through which the Mexican soldiers stormed. (See the photo of the modern Long Barracks on p.45.)

Now for the pièce de résistance. Exit the Covento Courtyard through the gate into the small plaza in front of the Alamo church – or, as the DRT prefers to call it, the "Shrine". Entering the front door of the church, you will encounter a bronze plaque with the following admonition:

> Be silent, friend
> Here heroes died
> To pave the way
> For other men.

Make no mistake; the Daughters mean it. They require that men remove hats and caps. Staff members graciously – but sternly – ask both voluble adults and boisterous children to speak in hushed tones. Remember, you're in a "shrine".

I do not mean to be as disdainful as that last statement may appear. Without being overly mystical, the site is extraordinary. Visitors feel its intensity as soon as they enter. Encased in those cold stones, one senses the presence of history. You cannot help but be aware that on this very spot, brave men fought and died. One must be a complete churl or an utter dullard, not to be moved by this place. It is, therefore, wholly appropriate that we show a measure of respect and, yes, even reverence.

Once inside the church one can view more artifacts. Among these is a long rifle used during the battle. Locals uncovered it soon after the fight and it is one of the few personal weapons historians can trace to the siege. Yet they have no clue as to which one of the defenders fired the piece. The noted Pennsylvania gunsmith Jacob Dickert crafted the longarm, thus its designation as the "Dickert rifle". Visitors can also view the cat's-eye ring that Travis wore during the siege. A buckskin vest that once belonged to Crockett is on display, as well as an 1830s Bowie knife. But the main attraction is the building itself. During the 1990s the DRT undertook extensive restoration to check the gradual deterioration of

the limestone. Their efforts were a smashing success and assured that the old church will stand for generations to come.

Passing through the side door of the church, visitors feed into the Gift Shop/Museum. Here they can find Alamo-related items to fit any interest or pocket. Souvenirs range from cheesy Alamo neckties to high-dollar collector items. And, of course, you can buy coonskin caps for the kids.

The Alamo Village

If you have time, make plans to visit The Alamo Village in Brackettville. It is the film set of John Wayne's 1960 epic *The Alamo.* It looks much more like the 1836 fort than the "shrine" in downtown San Antonio. It was also the set for *Alamo ... The Price of Freedom.* Having seen that film, one will have an increased appreciation for the reconstruction. Many say that they learned more about the battle from walking about this ersatz Alamo (which the initiated irreverently call the "Wayneamo") than they gleaned from the real one. Children especially enjoy The Alamo Village; here they can run on the walls and give their imaginations free rein without the atmosphere of stifling solemnity. It's a bit off the beaten path, but well worth the extra effort. Brackettville is located about ninety miles southwest of San Antonio on Highway 90.

Those planning a trip to The Alamo Village should check out its web site at: www.homestead.com/thealamovillage. One can phone at (830) 563-2580, or Fax at (830) 563-9226.

GOLIAD

The city web site will greatly assist those planning a trip to Goliad; its web address is www.goliad.org. Goliad is about 95 miles southeast of San Antonio at the junction of Highway 59 and Highway 183. The principal attraction is the Presidio La Bahía – which the Texians renamed Fort Defiance. La Bahía is the oldest fully restored *presidio* in the western United States. It is, furthermore, the only Texas Revolution site that maintains its 1836 appearance. The La Bahía complex consists of Our Lady of Loreto Chapel, a museum (originally the officers quarters), and the barracks. An 8ft stone wall encloses the compound.

Completed in 1779, Our Lady of Loreto Chapel is one of the oldest churches in the state. During the 1836 campaign, the Mexicans held their Texian prisoners in the chapel following the Battle of Coleto Creek. Fannin and the wounded were shot in the small plaza in front of the chapel. Today flags inside the chapel represent the state or country of origin of those who fell during the Goliad Massacre.

Each year the Presidio La Bahía schedules numerous living history programs. The largest takes place in March, when hundreds of living history devotees gather to reenact the Texian and Mexican occupation of the fort as well as the Goliad Massacre. In 2001, more than 4,500 spectators viewed the March living history presentations.

Those wishing to contact staff members at the Presidio La Bahía may do so by phone at (361) 645-3752, or by Fax at (361) 645-1706. The Presidio La Bahia is open daily, except at Christmas, Easter, and Thanksgiving, from 9.00am until 4.45pm.

Coleto Creek

While in Goliad be sure to visit the Fannin Battleground State Historic Site. It is located just outside the small community of Fannin about a mile south of Highway 59. Considering the significance of the Battle of Coleto Creek, the scant attention paid to this site will disappoint most visitors. In 1914 the state erected a 28ft granite monument. In 1965 the Texas Parks and Wildlife Department took over the maintenance of the site. A tiny, unmanned visitor center provides a brief introduction to the battle. Amenities include water fountains, restrooms, electricity, and a covered picnic area. The park encompasses only a small portion of the total battlefield, so visitors should also observe the land around the park as well. Fortunately, most of the ground adjoining the park is ranch land and remains relatively undisturbed. The park is open daily, but closes at 5.00pm

In many ways the lack of attention has been a blessing for the Coleto Creek battlefield. Unlike some Texas Revolution sites, this one has not been memorialized beyond recognition. The ground remains much as it was in 1836: flat, open, and forbidding. The downside is that visitors are quite on their own to interpret this battlefield. Even so, this book and the battlefield map on p.59 should prove valuable. Watch where you step! Rattlesnakes are frequent visitors to the site.

SAN JACINTO

San Jacinto Battleground State Historical Park, the site of the battle of San Jacinto, is some 20 miles east of downtown Houston. The park is located about 10 miles east of Pasadena, 5 miles northeast of the intersection of State highways 134 and 225. Houston traffic is vicious – avoid rush hours at all cost.

Arrive anywhere near the park and you will be able to see the mammoth San Jacinto Monument. It is a 570ft limestone shaft capped by a 34ft, 220-ton star denoting the Lone Star Republic.

The base of the monument houses a museum, which contains more than 100,000 artifacts, 250,000 documents, 10,000 visual images, and a library possessing 35,000 rare books. Be sure to catch the multi-image presentation, *Texas Forever!! The Battle of San Jacinto*. Narrated by Charlton Heston, the 35-minute production depicts the events of the Texas Revolution and the battle of San Jacinto. An elevator lifts visitors to an observation deck atop the monument. Before leaving the museum, be sure to visit the souvenir shop with its first-class book selection. The museum boasts a wonderful web site; pull it up at www.sanjacinto-museum.org.

The terrain is much altered from the time of the battle. The Houston Ship Channel obliterated much of the battlefield. Peggy's Lake is gone. Texans in their wisdom constructed the San Jacinto Monument directly over the site of the Mexican breastworks – arguably the most interesting portion of the battlefield. While impressive, the monument prevents military historians from ever fully investigating the original topography. This is another classic example of a monument obliterating the very ground it purports to celebrate. The Bird's-Eye View on pages 70-71 will help visitors achieve some notion of the battlefield's 1836 appearance.

While much of the original battlefield is lost, the Texas Parks and Wildlife Department has done an admirable job of marking the location of the Texian camp. One can see where the men of each unit pitched their tents. Recall that the battlefield was then – and is now – a swamp. Visitors, therefore, should come well armed with insect repellant. The mosquitoes are huge, plentiful … and thirsty.

The San Jacinto Battleground State Historical Park is open year-round, seven days a week from 8.00am to 9.00pm (1 March through 31 October), and from 8.00am to 7.00pm (1 November through 29 February). Facilities include restrooms, picnic tables, and concession facilities. There is no fee to enter the grounds. For additional information phone (281) 479-2421.

BIBLIOGRAPHY

Coleman, Robert M., *Houston Displayed; or, Who Won the Battle of San Jacinto? By a Farmer in the Army, Reproduced From the Original*. Intro. by John H. Jenkins. (1837; reprinted Austin, 1964)

Davis, William C., *Three Roads to the Alamo: The Lives and Fortunes of David Crockett, James Bowie, and William Barret Travis* (New York, 1998)

Duval, John C., *Early Times in Texas or, the Adventures of Jack Dobell*. Ed. by Mabel Major and Rebecca W, Smith (1936; reprinted Lincoln, 1986)

Filisola, Vicente, *Memoirs for the History of the War in Texas*. 2 vols. Trans. By Wallace Woolsey (1849; reprinted Austin, 1986, 1987)

Hardin, Stephen L., ed. *Lone Star: The Republic of Texas, 1836–1846* (Carlisle, Massachusetts, 1998)

Hardin, Stephen L., *Texian Iliad: A Military History of the Texas Revolution, 1835–1836* (Austin, 1994)

Hardin, Stephen L., *The Texas Rangers* (London, 1991)

Haythornthwaite, Philip, *The Alamo and the War of Texan Independence 1835–36* (Osprey, Men-at-Arms 173, 1986)

Huffines, Alan C., *Blood of Noble Men: The Alamo Siege & Battle, An Illustrated Chronology*. Illustrated by Gary S. Zaboly. Foreword by Stephen L. Hardin (Austin, 1999)

Jenkins, John H., ed. *The Papers of the Texas Revolution, 1835-1836*. 10 vols. (Austin, 1973)

Lack, Paul D., *The Texas Revolutionary Experience: A Political and Social History* (College Station, Texas, 1992)

Lester, Charles Edwards, *The Life of Sam Houston: The Only Authentic Memoir of Him Ever Published* (New York, 1855)

Maberry, Robert T., *Texas Flags* (College Station, Texas, to be published 2002)

Neito, Angelina, Joseph Hefter, and Mrs. John Nicholas Brown, *El Soldado Mexicano, 1837-1847: Organización, Vestuario, Equip*. (Mexico City, 1958)

Peña, José Enrique de la, *With Santa Anna in Texas: A Personal Narrative of the Revolution*. Expanded edition. Trans. and ed. by Carmen Perry. Intro. by James E. Crisp (College Station, Texas, 1997)

Roberts, Randy, and James S. Olsen. *A Line in the Sand: The Alamo in Blood and Memory* (New York, 2001)

Schoelwer, Susan Prendergast, with Tom W. Gläser. *Alamo Images: Changing Perceptions of a Texas Experience* (Dallas, 1985)

Thompson, Frank. *The Alamo: A Cultural History* (Dallas, 2001)

INDEX